THE
GOSPEL
ACCORDING
TO
STARBUCKS®

Praise for
The Gospel According to Starbucks

"Cultural barista Leonard Sweet serves up a triple venti cup of relevant insights to wake up decaffeinated Christians. Careful, the book you're about to enjoy is extremely hot."

—BEN YOUNG, pastor and author of *Why Mike's Not a Christian*

"Reading this book is a caffeine jolt. Get ready to be accelerated into the future, with Jesus a central part of the experience."

—DAN KIMBALL, pastor and author of *The Emerging Church*
and *They Like Jesus, but Not the Church*

"*The Gospel According to Starbucks* inspires us to quit playing safe and mediocre lives and to fulfill our God-given potential. Leonard Sweet uncovers God's purpose for people not just as individuals but also as communities. An outstanding and thought-provoking book."

—PAUL MCGEE, international speaker and best-selling
author of *S.U.M.O. (Shut Up, Move On)*

"I have a massive passion for passion. It's my favorite spiritual topic. And I have a nominal coffee obsession, Starbucks being my ritual more often than not. So what a treat to read Leonard Sweet's extra-shot weaving together of the two—all in the hope that each of us will drink in the meaningful and passion-filled life we were designed for."

—MARK OESTREICHER, president of Youth Specialties

Praise for
The Three Hardest Words in the World to Get Right
by Leonard Sweet

"This book demonstrates that one of the seminal Christian thinkers in the postmodern era can also be a pastor. Leonard Sweet gets us to examine what it takes to live out love in this world, and he does it beautifully."

—TONY CAMPOLO, coauthor of *Adventures in Missing the Point* and professor of sociology at Eastern University

"Len Sweet has, in his inimitable style, tackled the three easiest-hardest words in the English language, wrestled them to the ground, hugged them, and then let them fly again. His imagination takes us on a journey, his mind is an encyclopedia of wonderful references, and his language is captivating. This book is a joy...and a challenge."

—TONY JONES, national coordinator of Emergent-US and author of *The Sacred Way*

"In *The Three Hardest Words*, Leonard Sweet plumbs the depths of Christianity to explore the richness of God's story, one that is abundant in love. As usual, Sweet's work is thought-provoking, insightful, and a must-read for any postmodern thinker."

—MARGARET FEINBERG, author of *Twentysomething* and *What the Heck Am I Going to Do with My Life?*

"It turns out that Jesus' simplest and most basic command—that we are to love one another—is the hardest one for us to live out. Leonard Sweet's book is a tremendous help in guiding us not only to say the words 'I love you' with greater understanding of what they really mean, but also to live them with greater integrity and intention."

—RUTH HALEY BARTON, cofounder of the Transforming Center and author of *Sacred Rhythms*

THE
GOSPEL
ACCORDING
TO
STARBUCKS®

Living
with a Grande
Passion

LEONARD SWEET

With Questions for Coaching and Conversation
by Edward Hammett

WATERBROOK
PRESS

THE GOSPEL ACCORDING TO STARBUCKS
PUBLISHED BY WATERBROOK PRESS
12265 Oracle Boulevard, Suite 200
Colorado Springs, Colorado 80921
A division of Random House Inc.

This book has not been prepared, approved, authorized, or licensed by Starbucks Coffee Company.

ISBN 978-1-57856-649-5

Library of Congress Cataloging-in-Publication Data
Sweet, Leonard I.
    The Gospel according to Starbucks : living with a grande passion / Leonard Sweet ; with questions for coaching and conversation by Edward Hammett. — 1st ed.
        p. cm.
    Includes bibliographical references.
    ISBN-13: 978-1-57856-649-5
    1. Spiritual life—Christianity. 2. Coffee habit—Miscellanea. 3. Starbucks Coffee Company—Miscellanea. I. Hammett, Edward H. II. Title.
    BV4501.3.S93 2007
    248.4—dc22

                                        2006031244

Printed in the United States of America

2007
10 9 8 7 6 5

SPECIAL SALES
Most WaterBrook books are available in special quantity discounts when purchased in bulk by corporations, organizations, and special interest groups. Custom imprinting or excerpting can also be done to fit special needs. For information, please e-mail SpecialMarkets@WaterBrookPress.com or call 1-800-603-7051.

To Ron Lee,
editor and friend.

Contents

ACKNOWLEDGMENTS

*L*ife is hard enough with coffee. What would life be without coffee? Or without friends to enjoy coffee with? Friends such as Greg Glatz, Peter Walker, and Russ Wills gave me honest appraisals of my work and saved me from falling into many two-handed traps ("on the one hand/on the other hand"). They also kept me kicking a problem around when I wanted to punt and move on. Tim Schraeder of Riverside Community Church in Peoria, Illinois, let me read the training manuals for Starbucks's baristas.

This book is my personal attempt at updating the medieval method of reading for the four senses of Scripture (literal, allegorical, tropological, and analogical) and applying these four senses to the reading of culture. For helping me decide what to keep and what to discard, special thanks go to my friend Eddie Hammett, who appeared on the screen or in person to keep me shoveling. Eddie is a popular coach, coach trainer, and seminar leader for various seminaries, denominations, and judicatories. He wrote the "Questions for Coaching and Conversation" that you'll find in the discussion guide near the back of this book. A greater number of these questions, designed to help you go even deeper into grande passion and EPIC faith, can be found online both at Eddie's Web site (www.transformingsolutions.org and www.thecolumbiapartnership.org) and at mine (www.leonardsweet.com).

As I was finishing this book, I picked up Jonathan Petropoulos's work on Hitler and the German princes (*Royals and the Reich: The Princes von Hessen in Nazi Germany* [2006]). These members of the nobility comprised one of the two "professional" groups that most supported Hitler en masse (the other being physicians). In his acknowledgments, Petropoulos thanked his eleven (that's right, *eleven!*) research assistants. My first reaction was to float a fantasy about what life might be like with eleven research assistants. Then I realized that I already have more than eleven research assistants, bundled in one person by the name of Betty O'Brien. I wouldn't trade any eleven for one Betty.

A reader has the benefit of enjoying the work of a writer without having the bother of putting up with the writer himself. I thank Elizabeth and my three kids still living at home (Thane, Soren, Egil) for putting up with a lot of blank stares and "say that again."

I also want to thank my editor, Ron Lee, who intervenes at times to save me from myself. Ron has done this over and over again in the course of the three books he has edited on my behalf. Every time I called him, he sounded excited to hear from me. Every time I sent him a draft, he enthused about what I was writing, even while slashing away when my words were more adolescent than luminescent and straightening out my logic, which often is less linear than cousinly. In my life, Ron has graduated from being my editor to being my friend.

The Bible is right. You can't live by bread alone. You need apple butter on your bread, you need coffee in your cup, and you need a friend like Ron Lee to enjoy it with.

Introduction

The Brew of the Soul

Your Spiritual Life on Drip

How do you take yours?

Chances are that you take it some way. I know I do. I'm an eight-a-day "cupper." And even at that, I'm a wuss in my "attachment" (a Buddhist usage that I feel works much better than *addiction*). At least when my habit is compared to the eighteenth-century composer Johann Sebastian Bach, the eighteenth-century philosopher Voltaire, and especially the nineteenth-century French novelist Balzac (called by Baudelaire "the novelist of energy and will"),[1] who drank more than fifty cups of coffee a day. (He died at age fifty, some say from caffeine poisoning.)

People around the world drink more coffee than any other drink besides water: four hundred billion cups a year. And more people are drinking more coffee more frequently with every passing year.[2] Second only to oil as a USAmerican import, coffee is the drug of choice for the majority of North Americans, with 167 million USAmerican coffee drinkers alone quaffing five million tons a year in this nineteen-billion-dollar industry.[3] The average coffee drinker admits to 3.4 cups a day. But remember: a "small" Starbucks cup is "tall."[4]

Looked at another way, every USAmerican over eighteen years of age swills one and four-fifths cups of coffee a day.[6] But compared to either the Viennese or Swiss, we're teetotalers. Our per capita consumption of more than ten pounds of coffee beans per year[7] looks puny compared to the Austrians (14 pounds) or the Swiss (15.5 pounds). In the Netherlands, each citizen (birth to nursing home) downs on average an amazing four cups a day.[8]

> Coffee, according to the women of Denmark, is to the body what the Word of the Lord is to the soul.
>
> —ISAK DINESEN[5]

A HEALTHFUL JOLT OF JAVA

Of course, coffee consumption in USAmerica pales in comparison to soft drinks (70 percent of which are carbonated). Soda pop and other such beverages add up to 574 cans for every man, woman, and child. But unlike soda's sugar high, java jolts are actually good for you. Historically, physicians have been of two minds about caffeine. When they were not warning of its harmful effects, they were prescribing coffee for healthful impact on an astounding variety of diseases—from kidney stones and gout to smallpox, measles, and coughs. Now that sophisticated studies are being conducted to find out the real impact of caffeine, it seems the harder researchers work to detect the bad things coffee does to you, the more they unearth coffee's health benefits.

> Coffee should be black as Hell, strong as death, and sweet as love.
>
> —TURKISH PROVERB[9]

It is known, for instance, that coffee delivers more health-giving antioxidants to our diet than fruit, vegetables, and nuts.[10] At six cups a day and under, coffee reduces your chance of getting Parkinson's disease, liver and colon cancer, cirrhosis of the liver, Type 2 diabetes, and, if you are a fast metabolizer, heart disease.[11] As a bonus, coffee improves male fertility.[12] Caffeine can also protect you against skin cancer—but you'd have to smear it on your body for it to work.

COFFEE AND YOUR SOUL

Unlike soda, coffee improves creativity, fights fatigue, and has a long half life (six hours). Just ask a college student.[13] Also unlike soda, coffee is a hospitality drink, a sign of welcome and openness to sharing. There are few things I enjoy more in life than what I call soulcafés: sharing good stories over good coffee.[14]

I've had my share of bad stories over bad coffee too. But either way, a soulcafé represents some of the most memorable moments of my life. I've had soulcafés with mysterious brews I call airport coffee over vinyl tablecloths, hospital coffee over waiting-room chairs, cowboy coffee over bare picnic tables, and

> *A cup of coffee commits one to forty years of friendship.*
> —TURKISH PROVERB[15]

thermos coffee over workshop benches. My favorite soulcafé is communion coffee, which fuels passionate brainstorms with other dreamers and schemers. Coffee talk makes the best God talk.

It will come as no surprise that my coffee of choice is Starbucks, not just because they brew a superior variety of coffee but because of the experience that comes with the drink. You can enjoy Starbucks alone, but it's preferable to go there with a friend.

Starbucks Coffee Company is arguably the number one corporate success story of the last quarter century. Its stock is up 5,775 percent since it went public in 1992.[16] Some call Starbucks "Fourbucks" because that's what they usually end up spending there. But customers flock to Starbucks not to stand in line so they can pay three or four bucks for a cup of coffee. They pay so they can enjoy the Starbucks experience. The value comes with the experience that surrounds the cup of coffee. Starbucks lovers connect with the warmth of friends as they enjoy the warmth of their favorite drink.

A SENSORY FEAST

If you're a fan of Starbucks, you know what I'm talking about. You walk in and are greeted by rich, opaque colors from every angle. In the background, appealing music thick with atmosphere refrains from masking the almost whistle of the espresso machine. Dim lighting keeps the mood relaxed but suggestive, and a medley of complex coffee smells ooze from every surface you touch. In a number of ways, Starbucks is a three-dollar sensory feast.

In this book we will examine the Starbucks experience not simply so we can talk about coffee or the four million coffee drinks that Starbucks sells daily in USAmerica, but so we can learn what Starbucks has come close to perfecting—that life is meant to be lived with passion, and that passion is found and practiced through experiences, connection, symbols and images, and the full participation of every part of your being. Not only do these simple truths explain the phenomenal growth of Starbucks Coffee Company, they also point out the blind spots, weaknesses, and failures of the church to serve people at the level of life's bottom line: passion and meaning.

Let's be honest: *life* is a loaded word. It can mean everything from resignation ("Well, that's life.") to exhilaration ("I love life!"). The ancient Greek language helps us here. Like the four Greek words for *love,* Greek also has many words for *life.* In this book, we'll examine what I have coined the EPIC life, which in Greek is the word *zoe.* (We're not concerned here with the life of mere existence, *bios.*) Zoe means flamboyant, passionate life. Or in the words of Jesus: "I have come that they may have *zoe,* and have it to the full."[17]

Jesus recommended that his disciples learn something from the wisdom of the world. He observed that "the people of this world" pursue their dreams with greater passion and intelligence than "the people of the light."[18] One of my favorite theologians, Augustine of Hippo, made the case for finding bona fide beauty in the world (forged in the light of his own struggle with Manichaeism), all of which underscores the wisdom of keeping our eyes open to the truth that surrounds us.

A DRINK OF PASSION AND A PASSIONATE FAITH

With almost every study, it seems, we are discovering that fewer USAmericans than was previously thought attend church. Organized religion has been assuming that because it has a better product—namely, God—that it simply needs to open the doors and customers will line up. That assumption no longer holds.

Christians have much to learn about faith as a lived experience, not a thought experiment. Rational faith—the form of Christianity that relies on argument, logic, and apologetics to establish and defend its rightness—has failed miserably in meeting people where they live. Intellectual arguments over doctrine and theology are fine for divinity school, but they lose impact at the level of daily life experience. Starbucks knows that people live for engagement, connection, symbols, and meaningful experiences. If you read the Bible, you'll see that the people of God throughout history have known the same thing. Life at its very best is a passionate experience, not a doctoral dissertation. The problem is not that Christianity can't be believed, but that it can't be practiced because of its lack of lived experience. And it can't be observed by others because there are too few Christians who are radical enough to manifest what the gospel really looks like.

The church has not always been so disconnected from the raw elements of life. And it's entirely possible for people of faith to get back to the elementary, elemental aspects of their faith, their spirituality, and the gospel they proclaim. The question is, How?

As a beginning point in answering that question, let's examine a tangible and compelling example: the philosophy and practices of Starbucks Coffee Company. Let me issue an invitation to learn (or in some cases, to relearn) how to meet God in an irresistible experience, how to trade religious duty for spiritual passion, and how to engage in the life of faith in close relationship with other wayfarers.

It's time to take seriously the first and last commands of the Bible: eat freely[19] and drink freely.[20] If you can wait until I pour myself a fresh cup of Christmas Blend (my very favorite), we'll begin to do just that.

One

Reading a Starbucks Cup

Why Spirituality Is Going to Pot

The children of this world are in their
generation wiser than the children of light.
—Jesus[1]

*B*efore I ask you to read any further in this book, I'm going ask you to
read something else: a Starbucks cup. I could have picked a number of
other things for you to read: an ice-cream cone from Cold Stone Creamery
("Starbucks for kids"),[2] or a dining-room table from Ikea,[3] or a NASCAR[4]
race car, or any episode of *American Idol, Lost,* or *24.* Or, for that matter, any
two-hour performance of Blue Man Group.

But since I'm writing the book, I get to pick what we use as our text. And
I choose a Starbucks cup. The philosopher and critic Jacques Derrida is perhaps most known for his axiom, "All the world's a text."[5] We can read all of
our experiences as textual signs.

Do you have our text in hand? Go ahead and pick up a Starbucks cup.

What you're holding speaks volumes about the significance of what this book is about: a grande gospel, a frappuccino faith, a venti life of romance and passion. It's nothing less than the gospel according to Starbucks.

Starbucks views its brand as a kind of cultural portal. I propose to use it as a kind of spiritual portal. Christians can gain unexpected insight (like a surprise affogato shot to top it off!) into the life-enhancing power of the gospel by reading a Starbucks cup. The cup itself—and what's inside—can tell you about the deeper meaning of a spiritual life. Jesus, while not a coffee drinker, modeled the life of faith as both a consuming philosophy and a daily practice—a full-life engagement. He showed us that it's a life in which God is as immediate, available, and real as a steaming cup of coffee first thing in the morning. Life with God: it's "the best part of wakin' up!" (with thanks to Folgers for their tagline).

BREWED FOR THOUGHT

If you could get together with just one person from history for coffee and conversation (other than Jesus), whom would it be? Why that person?

Do you think Jesus ever got bored? If he did, it's not mentioned in Scripture. I tend to think he was so engaged in life that he never had a chance to taste boredom. In fact, a case could be made that the ultimate spiritual taboo for a disciple of Jesus is boredom, especially boredom brought on by a didactic approach to faith. Jesus practiced a way of living that was visceral, vibrant, and vigilant with meaning. His way of truth was a way of living. And his way of living is one that you or I would gladly stand in line for, and ultimately give our lives for.

Jesus did not endure his days on earth out of a sense of obligation. His life was characterized by joy and energy; it was spent in relationship with others. Today, too many Christians line up to follow God out of duty or guilt, or even hoping to win a ticket to heaven. They completely miss the warmth and richness of the experience of living with God. They fail to pick up the aroma of what God is doing in their part of town.

Here's the truth: God has set up shop where you live. The doors are open and the coffee is brewing. God is serving the refreshing antidote to the conventional, unsatisfying, arms-length spiritual life—and God invites you in. God won't make you stand in line.

When this is stated in words it's easy to miss the impact of all that it means for us. That's why I've written this book with your local Starbucks in mind. (That's Starbucks plural, since there is very likely more than one in your town.) It's something that is easy to identify with and something that attracts thirty million customers a week. Let's see how the passion that Starbucks has for creating an irresistible experience can connect you with God's stirring introduction to the experience of faith. By the time you finish this book, you'll see that the cup of coffee you enjoy in the morning is much closer to a chalice of communion wine than you realize.

Morning Fix at Six

If what we're really talking about is the biblical meaning of life with God, why resort to looking at a chain of coffee shops? Well, for several good reasons. Starbucks signifies passion and relationship and meaningful experiences. It also demonstrates the power of small numbers in our small and getting-smaller-every-day world. The power of one has never been greater. And biblically, the power of one person plus God cannot be surpassed on earth...not to mention the power of two people plus God.

For now, though, think of the power of one even *without* God. Think of Hitler, or Stalin, or Mao. It didn't take them hundreds of years to produce their own holocausts. It took only one lifetime for Mao to end the lives of well over seventy million in China![6] Not to mention Pinochet, Pol Pot, Idi Amin, and other twentieth-century tyrants. It only takes one. Small is the new large.

BREWED FOR THOUGHT

A joke in the nineties said there were two reasons why people visit Mao's mausoleum: to salute him and to confirm his death. Think about the historical figure you chose to meet for coffee. What did you talk about?

The power of one has been squared, or even cubed, by mediated culture. No empire is so large it can go it alone; no individual is so small that he or she cannot change the world. One bad egg with a bad attitude can spoil a face-to-face meeting. On a global scale, one person hiding out in a cave in the mountains bordering Afghanistan has the audacity to offer a "truce" with the most powerful nation on earth. One person declared war on USAmerica, and it's costing ninety-eight million taxpayers billions of dollars per year. Just ten thousand avowed terrorists at most, a tiny speck of the global population of six billion, have turned an entire planet into a panic. We are living in a world where very few can kill very many, where even one of us can kill all of us.

There also is a tremendous upside to the power of one. Who has had the greater impact for God and the gospel in the early twenty-first century? Any denomination with a million-plus members, or one musician named Bono? While you're debating the answer, think about a world with just one Starbucks coffee shop. That's right, just one.

JUST ONE STARBUCKS

The Starbucks phenomenon started in 1971 with one little store on a side street across from Seattle's farmers' market. In the early 1990s Starbucks was gunning for two thousand stores by 2000. By 2006 there were six thousand stores in USAmerica and four thousand overseas and in Canada. The goal for the number of Starbucks in USAmerica was set at ten thousand in 2002. As of this writing, the long-term goal for USAmerican stores is fifteen thousand, and the worldwide goal is thirty thousand.[7]

Anybody remember the Beirut of the 1970s? The images that stick in the mind are of bombed-out buildings and armored vehicles patrolling shell-shocked streets during the Lebanese civil war, which claimed up to one hundred seventy thousand lives, or one in twenty-five of the total population.

Until the 2006 Hezbollah shootout with Israel, Beirut was a bustling city with ten Starbucks.[8] There are more than one hundred Starbucks in Seoul, Korea, and Starbucks is taking China by storm (with four hundred already in the region). In 2006 Starbucks averaged five store openings per day in USAmerica and in thirty-seven countries around the world.

The refrain is real: "distance is dead." Any place can be every place.

HEAR THE TASTE OF COFFEE

Starbucks is expanding at an unheard-of rate, and one secret of its success is that Starbucks has a higher "contextual intelligence" than almost any other company. Think about this: a few years ago the world's largest chain of coffee shops received eight Grammys.[9] Eight music awards. Starbucks is a major player in the music industry, and Starbucks is now gunning for Oscars to add to its Grammys[10]—working with movie makers to produce a new line of movies. If you didn't hear about the feature film *Akeelah and the Bee* you must have been living under a rock...or drinking coffee crystals at home!

Starbucks has become an arbiter of pop culture, shaping popular tastes far beyond the flavor of a brewed drink. Starbucks is a lifestyle, not a coffee shop, a life house more than a coffeehouse.

But how and why did Starbucks become a leading purveyor of music and a shaper of USAmerican culture? Why all the noncoffee context surrounding the nation's leading coffee franchise?

One reason is that coffee is a conversation drink, and Starbucks knows that conversations need "third places" in which to thrive. And third places—which are not your office and not your home—need music and other media. Hence the unofficial Starbucks mission statement: to help people "Live More Musically." In Starbucks philosophy, when the music stops, life stops. Thus it is not by accident that Starbucks has become one of the most potent forces in the world of music, with a song library in the hundreds of thousands and a plan to put media bars in every Starbucks so you can shop for CDs or burn your own.[11]

BEAN THERE

Coffee boasts an impressively complex molecular makeup, with as many as four thousand discrete chemical constituents. The water used to brew the coffee contains as many as one hundred additional active components. Add bovine cream and you get another one thousand or so compounds and chemicals. The sugar (sucrose) sometimes used to sweeten coffee includes up to sixty different chemical entities. In terms of flavor molecules, only wine rivals the complexity of coffee. Even then, coffee is more complex than wine: eight hundred flavor molecules versus four hundred in red wine and two hundred in white.

Coffee, after all, is a sensory drink. The taste is bold, but that's just one part of the experience. Your senses feel the heat of the liquid inside, the steam rises to your face, the cup warms your hands. At Starbucks, music simply adds sound and rhythm to these other sensory experiences. Thus, a coffee company is creating a "Starbucks Sound," a recognizable brand of music that would never jar a cup of coffee.

PREACHER OF THE STARBUCKS GOSPEL

Starbucks has one of the best CEOs in the world. Howard Schultz sees himself, not as the Chief Executive Officer of Starbucks, but as its Chief Evangelist Officer. When he is asked to describe how he sees himself, Schultz sometimes responds, "I'm a coffee evangelist."[12]

For years, anyone who goes to church and also likes to read business books has watched corporate America appropriate the language of faith. I find it troubling that the world is stealing Christianity's best lines. From "mission statements" and "servant leadership" to "no fear," the world is co-opting the church's language.

BREWED FOR THOUGHT

Is nothing sacred? The Nike swoosh appropriates half of an ancient Christian symbol—a fish. You can try this at home: Draw a swoosh in the air, then flip it upside-down. Together these swooshes make the early Christian symbol.

But why has Christian language been co-opted by corporate America? Partly because the church doesn't know what to do with its own stuff. We can't figure out how to use it in this new world. Or in the words of science fiction writer Bruce Sterling, we've lost the ability to teach "old dogmas new tricks."[13]

I got bit by old dogma when I was asked to be considered for the E. Stanley Jones Chair of Evangelism at Drew University School of Theology. The seminary faculty unanimously supported my appointment. But without the personal intervention of Drew's president, my nomination might have floundered. Why? Because some members of the Board of Trustees were deeply troubled by the word *evangelism* and all that the word had come to stand for. It was felt that evangelism really meant "cultural imperialism," a religious excuse to mow down adherents of other religions in the name of the Lord—and to expand USAmerican influence at the same time.

Even a cursory look at history will show that the church didn't enter foreign lands bringing along nothing more than the Bible and a stirring testimony. Missionaries brought with them Western customs and mores that fell far short of the biblical standard. And often, Western culture was the least invasive product imported by missionaries. At times the military followed close behind, and in most cases Western economic interests were sure to discover the new frontier. Was evangelism simply a front for military expansion and economic exploitation?

If you shift your focus from world missions and look instead at evangelism as it has been practiced in our own nation and in our own time, it still holds true that the word has been sullied. The church has taught evangelism as a meeting of two antagonists—one righteous and right, the other dead wrong. The point of evangelism, according to this school of thought, is to win an argument. Evangelism also has been taught as a spiritual sales pitch, more nuanced perhaps than a religious argument but still relying on high pressure and ultimately committed to closing the deal. And if not an argument or a sales pitch, the gospel is neutered and reduced to an objective, nonrelational exercise in logic. The strategy is to convince others, not to appeal to them.

Somehow, the church lost touch with the meaning of *good news*. And why wouldn't Christians lose touch with the heart of the gospel? I've never met anyone who was energized by cliché one-liners and subcultural kitsch. But offer people a meaningful, earth-changing mission and then just *try* to hold them back! The Jesus example of meaning and passion over duty and obligation moves people. Starbucks understands this, and so should the church.

STARBUCKS EVANGELISM

As the controversy swirled at Drew University School of Theology over this word *evangelism*, and I saw how willing some Christians (even clergy) were to drop the term entirely, I began hearing the word spoken ever more loudly in some surprising places—namely the corporate world. Some of the biggest names in the worlds of science and business (Tim Berners-Lee, Kevin Kelly, Eric Raymond, Tom Peters, Guy Kawasaki, Jonathan Bulkeley) are now calling for leaders ("new revolutionaries") to become "evangelists" and "evangineers."[14]

BREWED FOR THOUGHT

The best and the brightest in the corporate world are proud to be known as evangelists. Why do you think the business world plugged into the power of evangelism just as the church seems to have lost the vision?

This is a shift of biblical proportion. Consider the following:

- Japan's hottest wireless phone vendor, Yasumitsu Shigeta, calls himself a "phone evangelist."[15]
- Larry Gibson is a former West Virginia mining maintenance worker who has done a turnaround. He now calls himself an "evangelist of the environmental cause."[16]

- John Bates, cofounder of BIGWORDS.com and Radionet, has a calling card that reads "John Bates, Evangelist," a job title that is increasingly common in the Web world. Karen Allen has the job title of "Internet Evangelist" for the Recording Industry Association of America.[17]
- One of six questions asked by Russell Reynolds Associates to determine whether you have "Web DNA" is, "Are you more evangelical than Matthew, Mark, Luke, or John?"[18]
- As part of its seventy-fifth anniversary celebration, *Business Week* presented a series of profiles of the greatest innovators of the past seventy-five years. They chose people from finance, government, science, technology, and management. The person they selected from management was John F. Welch Jr. The title they gave him was "Management Evangelist."[19]

PROCLAIMING BETTER NEWS

An evangelist, in a biblical setting, is a bearer of the gospel, a "story catcher"[20] of good news, a storyteller of the glory of God. The evangelists of the corporate world are proclaiming the gospel of the bottom line. The evangelists of the biblical world proclaim the gospel of the "morning line"—Jesus, the Bright and Morning Star. The evangelists of the corporate world announce, "I'm the center of the experience." The evangelists of the biblical world announce that Jesus is the center of the experience. Where Starbucks and its evangelists get the story right is in the context they create and the experiences they offer up with every steaming cup.

If you're a Christian and you're looking for a working definition of *evangelist* that has meaning for today, you need look no further than Jesus. He set the standard not just for passion and meaning, but also for delivering arresting images and irresistible experiences. He is Light, Living Water, the Path to

God, a Shepherd seeking lost sheep. He is Life itself. He told compelling stories, and he is the Story. Jesus did not call us to the static posture of intellectual assent; he did not die so that we could choose to agree to a statement of faith. He called us to follow, to experience life like never before, to share with others in the life of faith. Passion, meaning, imagery, experience. Each of those has tremendous meaning for an evangelist; each one is part of the good news of the gospel.

If the evangelists Matthew, Mark, Luke, or John were here, they would tell you that faith is not primarily a matter of belief. They would emphasize instead aspects of life that are closer to what we would call passion. They would describe faith as immersion and engagement, a full-on experience of life that is far bigger than everyday existence. They would depict life on an EPIC scale. When it comes to the life of faith, nothing less than that can tell the real story.

Two

Life on an EPIC Scale

Choose the Spiritual Life You Can Taste

The powers of a man's mind are directly
proportional to the quantity of coffee he drinks.
—Sir James Mackintosh (1765–1832)

*I*f the life of Jesus teaches us anything, it is that spiritual reality reverberates in the physical world. By "reverberates," I mean not just that it has
meaning, but that it has dimension and impact as well. The spiritual life is
not just an interesting religious idea, or a hoped-for berth in heaven. The spiritual life has earthly dimension—it is life that you can taste, and smell, and
touch, and see, and hear. It is reality.

Jesus never traveled more than eighty miles from his boyhood home, but
no one would accuse him of living on a small scale. With Jesus, even the
smallest act or the simplest story was done on a grande scale. God became
flesh and walked the earth. In Jesus, God made the spiritual physical. Jesus,
more than anyone else, shows us what it means to live with a grande passion.

Starbucks built an assumption-shattering business by selling an irresistible experience along with every cup of coffee. Likewise, the life of faith opens up a full life—not a new set of moral standards or a longer list of religious requirements. The spiritual life is grande passion—life on an EPIC scale. You don't have to get by with the equivalent of truck-stop coffee that has cooked on the burner all night. You can enjoy the daily refreshment of the EPIC life—the passionate brew of the soul.

LIFE ON AN EPIC SCALE

The EPIC life is built on four essential elements: Experience, Participation, Images that throb with meaning, and Connection. Which is a bigger stretch: (a) corporate America appropriating the language of evangelism or (b) Christians getting in touch with experiencing God? If the business world can sense the importance and impact of "proclaiming the gospel," then Christians can recapture the life that touches God and that God touches, which has gotten lost in an era of overthinking the details of right living.

GROUNDS FOR TRUTH

If you grew up in the church, you might have been taught that passion is sinful. The spiritual passion that is evidenced by a consuming desire for God might have gotten obscured by all the warnings against lust, envy, pride, and greed, as if passion were concerned *only* with the satisfaction of sinful appetites. Don't lose the full meaning of this word. A driving hunger for God is passion at its best. Give yourself the freedom to enjoy the excitement and adventure of pursuing God with all your spiritual passion.

If we learn one lesson from Starbucks, it is this: People don't go out of their way to search for hype and superficiality—those are free for the asking. Starbucks, more than most corporations, understands the irresistible attraction of authentic experience. Perhaps the leading corporate evangelists can help open the eyes of Christians to what we have lost. If faith is indeed a life (which it is) and not merely a course of study or an intriguing intellectual pursuit (which it was never meant to be), then faith is nothing less than the consuming experience of God. It is not a set of beliefs or even a lifestyle, but breath and pulse and life itself. It is the opposite of hype; it is heartbeat.

Starbucks, while not a purveyor of faith, certainly understands the difference between product (goods obtained through a business transaction) and pursuit (the passionate investment of life in higher values). A cup of coffee is a product; enjoying conversation with a friend over coffee is a pursuit. Starbucks gets it.

PASSION AND THE EPIC LIFE

The more we are pulled into virtual space by our cyberculture, the more we need to be brought back to earth by extreme experiences of reality (such as holding a hot cup of coffee while surfing the Web). Corporate evangelists understand what is involved in attracting attention (in the positive sense), instilling loyalty, and capturing passion.

Starbucks is opening five new stores every day not because coffee is a revolutionary new product or because it's a life-changing beverage. Starbucks's contextual intelligence tells them that digital and Net culture is producing a new epistemology that I call EPIC. The sound of Starbucks's steaming espresso machines is the sound of the tectonic plates of culture shifting with a force not felt for many years. Remember, EPIC is an acronym for Experiential, Participatory, Image-rich, Connective. Anything in business or in the church that is working in this emerging culture is becoming more EPIC.

A cyberworld filled with Web surfing and video games, blogs and chat rooms, does not demand less intellectual muscle but different kinds of brain-power and problem-solving skills. Digital culture is not less literary, but it requires different literary devices and writing styles, ones that are more EPIC.[1] The implications for the church of this new EPIC way of knowing and experiencing reality are tremendous.

To bring the EPIC life down to earth, we need look no further than a cup of coffee. Coffee is a catalyst for making good things happen. Starbucks took an old, unexciting standby—hot, dark liquid in a cup—and made it an EPIC beverage that millions of people feel they can't live without. That, in very few words, captures the contextual intelligence that Christians can gain from studying the Starbucks way of doing business.

In the Starbucks world, coffee sits at the center of an EPIC experience that attracts more and more people because it resonates with how people are now living in the world. Coffee is not life, of course, but it's part of a life context that we all seek. For Christians, all it takes for your passion to take over the world is turning your activities into EPIC-tivities.

The EPIC elements define the life that every person is seeking. I'm not talking only about Christians. I'm talking about humans. This is no superficial search for status or "bigger and better." Nor is this an Atkins diet, the One

GROUNDS FOR TRUTH

To turn your life into an EPIC adventure, you need four essentials. The EPIC life is characterized by these elements:

- It is **E**xperiential.
- It is **P**articipatory.
- It is **I**mage-rich.
- It is **C**onnective.

Minute Manager approach that tells you what to do and what to eat. The EPIC life is organic and unscripted, an apt description of the adventure of the gospel when the scriptural and the unscripted are joined together. More on that later, but for now let's get acquainted with the four elements of the EPIC life. (In the chapters that follow we will examine each one in depth.)

GOOD TO THE LAST DROPPING

Perhaps the best way to introduce EPIC is through the story of a coffee bean known as Kopi Luwak. Since 1990 I have published more than seven hundred sermons.[2] When asked, "What's your favorite sermon?" I duck the question by mentioning one by Oxford theologian and Dominican Herbert McCabe, my favorite preacher. But when pinned to the wall by being asked "What's *your* favorite sermon?" I mention one I delivered that is based on a coffee bean.

Here is the EPIC nature of this sermon. The Image of a coffee bean invites everyone's Participation in an Experience that Connects them to God and to each other. Here is how the sermon plays out:

When people enter the church they are handed little, white paper containers, each of which holds a coffee bean—the most costly coffee bean in the world. (It's an expensive sermon to preach.) Because it costs three hundred dollars a pound, they sell Kopi Luwak coffee by the ounce. Only one thousand pounds of this coffee, at most, make it to the world market every year. Kopi Luwak, the world's most exotic bean, comes from only one place on earth: the island of Sumatra in Indonesia in a region known as Java.[3]

After I invite people to smell the bean (a chocolaty aroma), taste it (nutty and bold), or do whatever they want to with it, I tell more of the story. The word *kopi* is Indonesian for "coffee." *Luwak* is Indonesian for the cat, a palm civet, that is involved in the process of harvesting this bean. About the size of a fox, a luwak is a nocturnal, fruit-eating cousin of the mongoose. The Juan Valdez of the animal kingdom, it roams at night over the island of Sumatra and only picks the most perfect, ripe coffee cherries to eat. It would rather starve than feast on an inferior bean. The civet cat then defecates the undigested coffee cherries in sausagelike links, and local harvesters dig in the rainforest floor and river banks looking for civet cat dung. They wash the clumps until only the beans are left, which then are dried in the sun.

After explaining that these beans are naturally processed through the digestive and elimination systems of a civet cat, only once have I had a person who had chewed the coffee bean rush out of the sanctuary to throw up.

When God Talks Trash

Kopi Luwak coffee has another name, which is unfit for use in polite company. So I've decided to name it after another animal, the small, lovable dog known as a Shih Tzu. This is Shih Tzu coffee.

Isn't it amazing how God works? In nature you see this over and over again. What is honey? The nectar of nature. But what else is honey? Nothing but bee Shih Tzu.

In Asian cultures, women use white paint to make themselves look more beautiful. Do you know the source of the paint that is so carefully applied to their faces? Nightingale Shih Tzu.

What do mushrooms grow in that makes them so succulent and tasty? You guessed it.

I love sardines. But ask the guy working at the fish market for a sardine, and you'll hear laughter. There is no such thing as a sardine fish. Sardine is a name given to trash fish that is packed together in a can. Sardines are fish Shih Tzu.

When grapes shrivel into raisins, half of the rotting juice gets gobbled up by fungi (also known as yeast), which then urinates alcohol into the bottle until it is full. When the alcohol content gets high enough it kills the yeast. In other words, the fungi drown in their own waste, and the ensuing product is called wine.[4] Wine is pee-juice: grape Shih Tzu.

GROUNDS FOR TRUTH

Christianity abounds in unexpected, upside-down, EPIC images. Take Ash Wednesday, the day Christians begin the forty days of Lent. What are the ashes that we put on our foreheads? Burnt garbage.

The dove is a beloved Christian image. But *dove* is nothing other than a poetic name for a trash bird called a pigeon. God chose a trash bird as the symbol of the Holy Spirit. We prettify it by calling it a dove, but really it's just a pigeon. And it doesn't stop with a trash bird used as a divine symbol.

Jesus grew up in a trash place called Nazareth ("Can anything good come from there?"[5]). Where was Jesus born? In a stable. What goes on in a stable? More Shih Tzu. What were Jesus' first smells as he entered this world? Animal waste.

What were Jesus' last smells as he experienced physical death? He was crucified at a place called Golgotha, which was the garbage dump for the city of Jerusalem. Jesus died smelling refuse.

THE GOSPEL UPSIDE-DOWN

Why do I make such a big deal about the odd appearance of animal waste and trash in the gospel accounts? Because the gospel is *the* EPIC account.

And this ultimate EPIC account tells us that living EPIC-ally isn't about being first or being strong. Rather, it's about being last, being humble, and losing—losing our lives to find life. What is most weak, most despised, and most contemptible in your life and mine can become, through the power of the Holy Spirit, what is most beautiful and most radiant, and what can produce the most blessing.

If you want to be first, you have to be willing to be last.

Do you want to be strong? You have to be willing to be weak.

Do you want to win? You have to be willing to lose.

An EPIC faith is an upside-down, topsy-turvy faith that shows that God can turn buried trash into buried treasure. The Hebrew word for "hell" was *Sheol.* Heaven was *Shiloh.* God can turn any Sheol into a Shiloh if you will let God take that pain, suffering, and ugliness and let God's Spirit turn it upside down. Treasure chests can be hammered out of trash cans.

In 1823, William Webb Ellis was a student at a British school called Rugby School. One day he was playing soccer and he had a brain cramp: instead of kicking the ball, he caught it. With the ball in his hands he ran to the goal, and all of a sudden, instead of hearing the cheering crowds, he heard the humiliating cries of a mocking crowd.

But someone who watched what Ellis had done with the ball on the soccer field saw treasure and not a mistake. The spectator used Ellis's mistake to create a different sport. He named it *rugby* after the school where it first appeared.[6] But the creation of a new sport did no good for William Ellis because he couldn't trust that a trash can could be hammered into a treasure chest.

The dominant story of the Scriptures, from Genesis to the maps, is the story of how God takes what is worst, least, and most contemptible and does what is greatest, best, and strongest. It is nothing less than the EPIC story of the gospel.

God's Power Demonstrated in Humiliation

What might easily be the most EPIC image in all of Scripture is also the ultimate insult. It is named in Numbers 12:14: to spit on someone. In ancient times to spit on another human, to curse somebody by spitting on him, was the insult to end all insults.

One of the most heartbreaking stories that came out of the civil rights movement involved an eight-year-old named Thelma. She was the first student to integrate the Mississippi public school system. Before she left for school on the first day, her mother dressed her in a cute pink dress. When Thelma showed up at school, the teacher said, "Thelma, I want you to stand right there by your seat. You are not to sit yet."

Thelma did as she was told. She stood as the rest of the third-grade class marched past and spat in her seat. After the other children reached their seats, the teacher instructed Thelma, "You can sit down now."[7]

Spitting is the ultimate symbol of insult. But what did Jesus do when he wanted to heal a blind man? He spat and then scooped up some dirt. He used his spittle in that earth to make a healing compound and transformed an activity of cursing and insult into an EPIC-tivity of healing and redemption.

Over and over again in the Bible, God turns cursing into curing; God turns belittling into blessing; God turns burrs into spurs. The curse of being hanged on a tree was transformed into the miraculous act of forgiveness and salvation.

From Rogue's Gallery to Hall of Saints

Here is a short list of gospel heroes, men and women who, on a human level, were the least and the worst. But in God's EPIC scheme, these same people were transformed into heroes:

- Moses was a murderer. He recycled his rage and became the greatest leader in Israel's history.
- Jacob was a schemer and a thief. He recycled his cunning and became Israel, the father of a nation.
- David was an adulterer. He recycled his passion and became the greatest of the Hebrew kings.
- Peter was a boastful, profane fisherman. He recycled his pride and became the rock upon which Christ built his church.
- Mary Magdalene recycled her undisciplined habits and became a passionate lover of God.
- Saul of Tarsus, a persecutor of Christians, recycled his hatred and became Paul, the greatest of the missionary theologians.
- Esther, a harem girl, recycled her sex appeal and saved the Jewish people from history's first Holocaust.
- Ruth was an idol worshiper. But she recycled her paganism and became a progenitor of Jesus the Christ.

If we learn to live the gospel like Starbucks lives coffee, then we will find God turning our trash into treasure, making our Sheols into Shilohs, and taking the worst out of our lives and turning it into the best.

BREWED FOR THOUGHT

Think about you. (I'll think about me.) What is "least" about you? Identify the dregs of your life. Now trust the EPIC gospel, which demonstrates that God wants to turn you upside down. God wants to take what is worst in you and turn it into a source of healing, wholeness, and redemption. That is how your ordinary, seemingly insignificant life can become an EPIC life.

The Civet Cat Coffee Bean Experience

When I finish preaching my favorite sermon, and I'm done playing with the rare and expensive Kopi Luwak coffee bean, I invite those who still have their beans to join me in the narthex of the church. If we are to experience the taste of the most expensive coffee in the world, we must pool our beans and grind them together. These coffee beans would not be expensive if people didn't relish the experience of Kopi Luwak—the coffee that is harvested from animal droppings.

A faith that is characterized by grande passion starts with meaningful experience. Imagine how different the Christian life would be if it was understood not as something to ponder or to observe in others—but as the one thing in life that has to be fully experienced. The EPIC life delivers the refreshing solution to theoretical Christianity. EPIC faith offers you a taste of life with God as you've never known it.

When you start living with EPIC (Experiential, Participatory, Image-rich, Connective) passion, your life takes on the aroma of God, the taste and feel of God, and it invites others to experience God for themselves. Understandably, it's difficult to picture such a departure from idea-based faith to visceral, full-on engagement with God. So in the chapters that follow we're going to look at the EPIC practices of Starbucks and then ask how the same principles might apply to the life of faith. I think you'll be surprised—and energized—by what we'll learn.

Your local Starbucks, on an admittedly limited scale, is the business-world equivalent of the irresistible experience that God invites you to enjoy. You can drink in the life of God and immerse yourself fully in what God is doing on earth. God offers arresting experiences that move you from obligation to passion, spilling over to benefit the lives of those who will see God become visible in your life.

All of this sounds good, but is it *true* with a capital T? Isn't it dangerous to place so much emphasis on *experiencing* God? Whenever I am interviewed, the question I'm almost always asked is this: "Dr. Sweet, do you believe in absolute truth?" There is only one answer: "I more than believe in it. I know Absolute Truth personally." Absolute Truth is Jesus.

The word *absolute* comes from the Latin *absolvere,* which means to "set free." Jesus said, "I am the...truth."[8] When we know the Truth, when we are in relationship with the Absolute, we will be absolved and set free to live EPIC-ally. To those who are failing at living, Jesus says, "You will know the truth, and the truth will set you free."[9]

The EPIC life is true with a capital *T.* It is the irresistible answer to lukewarm, colorless spirituality. It is God's freshly brewed antidote to the dutiful Christian life. Once you respond to God's stirring introduction to the full experience of faith, you'll find spiritual passion that you'd gladly stand in line for.

Three

Drinking In
the Starbucks Experience

Epic: Starbucks Is Experiential

> From the heart it has come,
> to the heart shall it go.
> —BEETHOVEN's inscription of his Mass[1]

W hy do people gladly spend three dollars on a drink that a decade ago they'd spend only fifty cents on? You don't need me to tell you that specialty coffee is expensive. We can pay more on one drink from Starbucks than a supermarket asks for a whole pound of coffee. A cup of coffee at Starbucks costs sixteen dollars a gallon.[2] It would be far cheaper to drink gasoline. And think about this: people actually wait in line to spend that kind of money on coffee.

Twenty-four percent of Starbucks's customers visit sixteen times per month.[3] No other fast-food chain can claim that success. An investment of ten thousand dollars twenty-five years ago, when specialty and flavored coffees accounted for less than 1 percent of the total USAmerican coffee market, would now be worth five million dollars.[4] By the way, that 1 percent of the market has now swelled to 35 percent.[5] Starbucks has forced fast-food chains to upgrade their coffee. You can now get espresso at McDonald's or Burger King, and specialty (Java Coast) coffee at I Can't Believe It's Yogurt!

GROUNDS FOR TRUTH

Even in past eras it was not unusual to dig deep into the pockets for foods of pleasure such as sugar, chocolate, coffee, and tea. In Victorian times, nearly 25 percent of a family's food and drink budget was spent on coffee, tea, and sugar.[6]

Specialty coffees being sold at fast-food establishments force us to ask: why are people today, even people from developing nations around the world, willing to spend this kind of money on a cup of coffee?[7]

YOU DON'T STAND IN LINE JUST FOR COFFEE

A cup of coffee fetches such a high price because people aren't buying a cup of coffee. They are buying an experience of coffee. Starbucks sells in-your-face coffee with aroma that grabs you by the nose two blocks away and drags you into the store for a multisensory but coherent coffee experience. And it's that experience that convinces you a cup of coffee is worth three dollars.

Starbucks didn't set out to reinvent coffee. They aimed to reinvent the coffee experience.

In fact, Starbucks makes their coffee so experiential they have to help you handle the experience (hence the "bra" or thermal "jacket" to protect your hands from the heat). When a fast-food chain gets sued for serving coffee so hot it can scald your skin, it issues an apology and pays out big bucks in damages. Starbucks doesn't apologize or settle, but passes out more thermal jackets and prints warnings on its cups: "extremely hot."

Maybe we should warn spiritual seekers in advance that Jesus is not for the faint of heart, instead of "cooling down" the gospel so we can all sip religion comfortably on cushioned, suburban pews. The gospel was not meant to be comfortable or safe. Jesus does not invite lukewarm faith, the brand practiced by the Church of Laodicea. Instead, God promises to spit the lukewarm out of God's mouth.[8]

DOOMED BY SATANIC MEDIOCRITY

Starbucks addressed a real Laodicean scandal in USAmerican culture. The problem that Starbucks solved was "the mediocrity of the middle"—in this case, stale to awful coffee. The 1950s and '60s dredged the dregs in taste, everything from pasty "wonder bread" to insipid "instant coffee"[9] that came in the form of Nescafé powder, Folgers crystals, Sanka freeze-dried pellets, and Hills Bros grounds. USAmerica had a dirty little secret that only immigrants knew: we served the worst coffee in the world. And in a worst-coffee country, where were you served the worst of the worst? The church.

- Starbucks is Picasso; Maxwell House is Maxwell Parrish.
- Starbucks is Henri Gorecki; Folgers is Henry Mancini.
- Starbucks is Michelangelo's "David"; Sanka is Daniel Edwards's "Monument to Pro-Life: The Birth of Sean Preston."
- Starbucks is Thomas Cole; Chock full o'Nuts is Thomas Kinkade.
- Starbucks is Grandma Moses; Hills Bros is Grandpa Jones.

Spiritual passion is grande, not lukewarm. The life of faith is a life spent following Jesus, and Jesus is not a two-dimensional, make-believe deity who does our bidding. He leads us into all-consuming experiences of life, and it is crucial that we recognize the irresistible appeal of authentic experience. If you focus on the coffee, you don't get it. When you buy a cup of coffee you are buying the *experience* of coffee. This is a metaphor not only for grande passion in life, but for passionate faith.

We miss the point when we focus our discussions of consumption only on physical goods. The major phenomenon of the twenty-first century is that the leading areas of consumption are less material than experiential: from eating out to e-tourism to education, from health to holidays. People today don't collect things so much as they collect experiences. It's not just the *best* coffee that draws me to Starbucks. It's the *best experience* of coffee. There is a cost that must be counted, but high costs bring high rewards.[10]

DO YOU NEED ROOM IN THE CUP FOR CREAM?

Weather forecasters aren't all that interested in whether tomorrow will *be* colder than today. They are much more interested in whether tomorrow will *feel* colder. Think about the wind-chill index, which factors in wind speed and humidity with the actual temperature to give television viewers a better idea of what the cold will feel like. For Starbucks it's not really about the coffee or the other "things" they sell. It's about experiences that resonate with you emotionally. They want your cup of coffee to feel right.

The highest resonance comes when an experience is authentic. It can't be manufactured, synthetic, forced. Starbucks launches new products, not on the basis of what market research reveals, but based on intuition: "We know when it feels right," says the company's head of marketing.[11]

This is what makes the Starbucks experience authentic rather than staged. In spite of being engineered to sell coffee, Starbucks does everything corporately possible not to create a preplanned compelling experience for the customer, but to help customers create experiences for themselves. Starbucks wants to help you experience from the heart something that you will enjoy and share with friends. And it works. It is the very thing that has won my trust and loyalty and makes me as passionate about Starbucks coffee as some bikers are about Harley-Davidson motorcycles.

Starbucks is far from alone in selling people an experience.[12] "The Caribou Coffee Experience" is how the handbook for that company refers to their products. Or take Tim Hortons in Canada. In many ways the Canadian equivalent of Starbucks, Tim Hortons doesn't sell coffee. They sell experiences of Canada. I have yet to be with a Canadian who hasn't told me the life story of hockey player Tim Horton as we waited in line for our drinks and donuts. To visit Tim Hortons is to experience what it means to be Canadian.

BREWED FOR THOUGHT

Think about the most enjoyable experience you've had in the past week. What was it about that experience that made it "feel right"? Who else was involved? What were the circumstances that contributed to everything coming together just right?

Kraft Foods, which owns Maxwell House, spent millions of dollars trying to understand Starbucks and imitate them. But no matter how much they tried and no matter how hard they worked, they couldn't do it. So they gave up. But why was Kraft Foods unable to "do Starbucks"? They couldn't comprehend, much less embrace, the EPIC nature of Starbucks culture. They could not transition to more experiential, participatory, image-rich, connective modes of production. They made coffee in huge vats, vats as big as silos. Starbucks made coffee in little urns, or in single cups. "How do you do that and make money?" Kraft executives asked as they shook their heads in disbelief.

The Cannibal Approach to Growth

"Good experiences for the soul" is the credo that made it possible for Starbucks to rewrite the textbooks about the great retailing no-no called cannibalizing. Have you noticed how often you see two Starbucks stores doing business across the street from each other? This was immortalized in the movie *Shrek 2*, when the giant gingerbread man lumbers his way to one Starbucks, only to have the horrified customers rush out of that store and into the other Starbucks across the street. In the little fishing village (Anacortes, Washington) where I catch the ferry to go home, within a couple of blocks of one another there are three Starbucks. I've seen some intersections with a Starbucks on three of the four corners.

This tongue-in-cheek headline appeared in the spoof tabloid, *The Onion:* "New Starbucks Opens in Rest Room of Existing Starbucks."[13] David Letterman did a "Top Ten Things You Didn't Know About the Space Shuttle," and one of them was that at either end of the spacecraft there was a Starbucks. The proliferation of Starbucks within a few blocks of one another is not a rare exception. Fully one-third of all new Starbucks stores in the past five years have cannibalized an established store. It started in 1988, when Howard Schultz visited the company's first international store in downtown Vancouver, British Columbia. Starbucks executives were worried that maybe Starbucks wouldn't find a warm reception in "Tim Hortons country." But when Schultz arrived at the store, he saw what every retailer dreams about: a busy store with long lines of twitching customers waiting for their coffee.

While his staff were congratulating each other for their success, the tsar of Starbucks complained that "nothing fails like success" and expressed panic at the peril the company was in. "Why can't you celebrate Starbucks's success?" his colleagues wanted to know. "Because this is not success; this is danger," Schultz replied. "Nobody is going to stand in long lines to pay big bucks for a luxury drink but once."[14]

Schultz realized the key to success was to cannibalize the Vancouver store, so he proposed opening a second store directly across the intersection. "It wasn't a different neighborhood, but it had a different vibe." Different sides of a street have different traffic patterns, and people are not going to consistently alter their rituals or delay their day for a luxury cup o' joe.[15]

Starbucks's biggest obsession is ensuring that no one has a bad experience at one of its stores.[16] Starbucks's definition of a bad experience? Waiting in a long line to spend a lot of money on a luxury drink.

STUCK IN THE MIDDLE WITH YOU

Since we're reading a Starbucks cup to find clues to the deeper EPIC meaning, what's the first thing we see? A Starbucks cup teaches us that we live in a culture with great gusto for experiences, a culture desperate to feel and understand everything with passionate intensity. In fact, it is these experiences that help people feel alive. Living in one's head is no longer a deep life but a shallow life. The hunger of the soul is for living in one's heart as much as living in one's head.

People don't want staged experiences; they hunger (and thirst) for the spontaneity of authentic experience in this time of transition. Mass-produced and prefabricated don't cut it. We're looking for authentic experiences of the moment. What makes an experience authentic? And do authentic experiences happen in the middle places or only at the extremes?

BREWED FOR THOUGHT

What factors made your most enjoyable experience of the week authentic? What kept it from seeming fabricated, forced, or synthetic?

Before we set out for the extremes, we have to ask what's so bad about the middle. The Midwest is a fine part of the country. I lived there for eleven years. Middle America in many ways is the backbone of our nation. But think about the middle in a different way. What is the worst thing that can happen to a passenger on an airplane? It's having to sit in the dreaded middle seat. In buses and on subways, people would rather stand than occupy that middle space. The only way to get passengers to sit in the middle is to put in armrests that establish borders on spatial territory. If you don't believe me, just Google "the decline of the middle," "the vanishing middle," "the loss of a center," or "the elusive middle ground."[17] See what you find.

The shunned middle teaches us about authentic experience and its irresistible attraction in the twenty-first century. Authentic experience does not flourish in the trampled soil of the anonymous masses. It grows instead in the rarified extremes, in the fertile mulch that's building at the two ends of the well curve. (That's not a typo. I wasn't going for *bell curve* and missed the *b* key.)

Avoidance of the middle explains why Starbucks does not sell a size called a medium. Medium is not a virtue. What is the emotional strength of being not large but not small either? Just sort of there in between…a medium. The strength has left the middle. The Via Media has become the

BREWED FOR THOUGHT

Most of us spent our growing-up years in the bell-curve world, where the bulk of the human population resided in the middle. But think about your personal aspirations when you were young. Did you dream about getting average grades, playing on an average team, and getting lost in the crowd? Even when the bell curve was said to be the norm, few people set a goal to carve a niche in the middle.

Via Mediocre, especially in a well-curve world, which is the land we live in, the post-bell-curve world.

The Maxwell House world was a mass world: mass media, mass communications, mass culture. When I was growing up, I was taught that the place to be was the center of the mass. To be at the heart of anything was to be at the center. Likewise, to be in the middle of things, Maxwell House thought, was to be in the catbird seat.

Maxwell House and the rest of the mass world organized itself according to a hump-shaped bell curve in which everything clustered in big middles, in massified averages. Sociologists even crowned this bell curve a normal distribution curve and assumed that everything in society would organize itself around this regularity. But today's world doesn't go for the anonymous hump in the middle.

WELL-CURVED EXPERIENCES, NOT BELL-CURVED

If you're dealing with either ball bearings or natural selection, the bell curve distribution will almost always be the norm. But Sir Francis Galton warned that conditions in the world of nature would deviate from the bell curve during periods of transition.[18] To Starbucks's credit, they realized that the latter days of the twentieth century were such a time of transition, as we have left a world of uniformity and entered a not-only-but-also world of "janiformity."[19]

Indeed, economic and social phenomena are following the well curve,[20] not the old bell curve. A Starbucks world is not one that caters to the lowest common denominator or the big middle. In a well-curve world, the middle drops out and the extremes grow fast and strong. A well-curve graph spikes up at either end and collapses in the middle; hence, the opposite of a bell in the shape of a well.

Today all middles are in trouble. Go ahead, try to name a vibrant center. I'll give you a minute to think about it... Well? I bet you can name hundreds of vibrant edges and vital extremes. But middles (middle-class, middle-management, mainline religion) are dead or dying. In fact, middle ground is at best fallow ground.

Nobody wants to be average or to have mass appeal. To call someone vanilla is an insult. Today, no company in its right mind would name itself General Motors or General Electric or General Foods. There is no general anything, no happy medium anymore. Both ends now play against the middle. In this mitosis of the middle where the ends are getting stacked, the liposuctioned middle is creating an hourglass society.

THE SINKING, STINKING MIDDLE

Evidence of the loss of the middle is all around us. Find me a kid who isn't entranced by nonstandard sports such as mountain biking, skateboarding, wave boarding, or rock climbing. Nobody wants to do regular anything. If you still don't believe me, consider the following:

- Sales for midsized televisions are sagging. But huge home theater systems are hot, matched only by sales of tiny cell phones with video screens.

- Organizations are getting bigger in size through mergers and acquisitions, and they are getting smaller in size via nonemployer businesses and self-employment.

- USAmerica is becoming more dynastic than dynamic. There is faster income growth at the top and bottom ranges, with the slowest income growth at the middle.

- There is rising affluence and rising poverty.[21] The world is becoming one of Uppers and Downers,[22] the Have-Gots and the Have-Nots. The poor are not only still with us. The poor are getting more with us. The rich are getting richer faster than the poor are escaping from poverty.[23] And to understand the power of the rich, consider this one statistic: in Manhattan, "the residents of just 20 streets on the east side of Central Park donated more money to the 2004 presidential campaigns than [donors in] all but five American states."[24]

- USAmerica is one of the most religious countries on the planet. Yet it nurtures an intellectual, cultural, and media establishment that is aggressively hostile toward religion, making USAmerica one of the most religiously inhospitable countries in the world.

- Money in the future will be in digital form and in local economic units or in the form of barter.[25]

Watching the Food Network While Working Out on a Treadmill

One example of how to bring the ends together in a well-curve world, and the benefits of a simultaneous engagement of both ends of the continuum, is the competing food habits of indulgence and wellness. "Contradictory consumers" are going in opposite directions at the same time. We go from Ben & Jerry's Ice Cream or Krispy Kreme Doughnuts to the organic salad bar or raw juice bar. Or we stay at the Venetian Resort Hotel Casino in Las Vegas, where in the evening there is the decadence and extravagance of the Tao Nightclub, while during the day there is the Canyon Ranch SpaClub—both of which are trumpeted as spiritual experiences.

We live in a Godiva culture of indulgence layered upon indulgence lathered with a whipped-cream topping of guilty pleasures and a final red cherry of repentance. This is also a culture obsessed with weight and health consciousness. We have the highest obesity rates in the world, and eating disorders run rampant. How do you bring these "dueling extremes"[26] of death-by-chocolates and squeaky-clean foods together?

The blended, cut-to-the-middle solution of the bell-curve world was to introduce low-cal, low-fat chocolate. That didn't work. Why eat chocolate if you can't enjoy the fat-drenched flavor of decadence? People want the experience of luxurious chocolate. They don't want halfway, diluted experiences of chocolate. But they also want a responsible weight-management program, one that can make a difference and not just create delusions of health.

The key is to offer consumers two opposite experiences at the same time.[27] Hence portion-controlled chocolates. Nestlé's Butterfinger Stixx and Hershey's Sticks offer the binge experience of chocolate in a way that doesn't adversely impact the body. Hershey's Sticks, with a tagline promising a "convenient guilt-free way to indulge in chocolate," is available in an eleven-gram, sixty-calorie bar, with a choice of milk, dark, caramel, or mint-flavored chocolate.[28] In a similar vein, Nabisco has introduced 100 Calorie Packs (portion-control versions of indulgent snacks such as Oreos and Cheese Nips). Other companies are getting the idea. Have you noticed that miniature muffins, dwarf bagels, and one-hundred-calorie cookie bags are popping up everywhere?

Fed Up

The commerce of experience has its limitations, however. The search for meaningful experience (whether chocolate or religious) can be part of the problem as much as it's part of the solution. Too many good experiences can be bad for you. If there were an Academy Awards category for tastiness, Starbucks's Strawberry and Cream Frappuccino would get an Oscar. It offers an experience of strawberriness that is as close to freshly picked strawberries as you can get. But these strawberry experiences come with 770 calories and 19 grams of fat. Someone has calculated that a Strawberry and Cream Frappuccino packs the nutritional equivalent of a whole Pizza Hut Personal Pan Pepperoni Pizza that you sip through a straw.

This is not all that different from worship "experiences" that can quickly become monsters that need to be fed increasingly elaborate meals every week, and the preacher and worship team become the food. All of this leads to severe obesity—in more ways than one.

Authentic Experience

The product is no longer king, it's the experience that surrounds the product that brings people in the door. It can't be just any experience, though. Like the hated middle, people shun a manufactured, forced, commercial experience. But deliver an authentic experience of emotional strength, spontaneity, and simultaneity, and they'll stand in line for it.

That's why people crowd your local Starbucks. Coffee as a beverage might be worth only fifty cents. But coffee as an experience—especially in our well-curve world—that is easily worth several dollars. And not just today, but several times a week.

When was the last time you saw people lined up on Sunday morning to get into a church? It has probably been a while, and keep in mind that people don't have to pay to get the full treatment at church. What's missing, and what can individual Christians and the church at large learn about authentic experience from Starbucks? With the middle dropping out and the extremes growing, what does that tell us about faith and its connection to life for those seeking the ultimate authentic experience?

Four

The Gospel
in an Experiential Cup

*Living at the Intersection of Faith
and Irresistible Experience*

> Our house was not unsentient matter—it had
> a heart, and a soul, and eyes to see with;...it was
> of us, and we were in its confidence, and lived
> in its grace, and in the peace of its benediction.
> —MARK TWAIN on his home
> in Hartford, Connecticut[1]

The basic question of life is this: is God a reality to be experienced or a belief to be remembered? The basic question of the Christian life is this: is Christ a living force to be experienced or a historical figure to be reckoned with?

The Bible is less a book about how people thought about God than it is a book about the religious experiences of individuals and communities. Experience is the engine room of the biblical and spiritual enterprise. At least the Westminster Catechism thinks so. Since 1647, the first question that every Calvinist child has learned to answer is this one: "What is the chief and highest end of man?" The answer is equally famous: "Man's chief and highest end is to glorify God, and fully to enjoy him forever."

The EPIC life of faith begins with authentic experience. Do you honor the experiences of life God gives you by enjoying them? Can you sing praises for that bag of beans, that pot of Robusto, or that vanilla latte shampooed with latte art? Can you cry hosannas for intimate conversations over coffee? God is at work and at play in your life, sending you experiences of God. The stuff of divine revelation is experience—experiences that form themselves into story and story into theology.

> *A successful brand is ultimately a question of authenticity.*
> —STEFANO MARZANO
> of Philips Design[2]

The "Experience God!" story is not the end of the story, certainly, nor the complete story. But without the experience of delight and enjoyment, the life of faith is not a life but a theory. It is a deadening doctrine, not an enlivening discipline. It is a faint memory of something in the distant past and not a living reality of one's daily life today. You can have intellectual belief but be without EPIC faith.

People are starved for experiences that ring true, not just ring cash registers. Authentic experience is the starting point for a lived faith that not only transforms the individual, but also changes the world.

THE HOLY TRINITY OF AUTHENTICITY

One of my favorite television shows is PBS's *Antiques Roadshow*. The celebrity experts they consult to determine the authenticity of an item refer to the "holy trinity" of authenticity. For an antique to be authentic, it must pass muster with three intangibles: (1) provenance, (2) beauty, and (3) rarity. The triangulation of these three weightless assets creates an authentic work of art that is valued monetarily in five, six, or sometimes even seven figures, but most often is valued in deeper terms: "I wouldn't sell this for the world."

When I conduct advances at my home on Orcas Island, I have my own trinitarian authenticity drill. One of my favorite exercises is to gather all the advancers around the dining table and invite them to look upward at the chandelier. I begin with its provenance: it was crafted by the Quezal Art Glass and Decorating Company, founded in 1902 by Martin Bach and several others. Martin Bach was one of the best glassblowers at Tiffany studios when he left to form his own company. They chose the name Quezal to honor God's rambunctious artistry manifested in the brilliantly colored Central American bird known as the quetzal.

I then give the advancers a little test of their ability to discern beauty and rarity. Five of the tulip shades on the chandelier were created by one of Quezal's master glassblowers and are individually signed *Quezal* on the blunted blade of the shade. One was done by an apprentice and is unsigned. The beauty and rarity test? Find the unsigned shade.

About half can pick out the unsigned shade, but it takes a while. And it takes eyes that can see and senses that can discern the difference between glass that is merely pretty, and glass that is singularly iridescent with an almost magical quality of inward-burning translucence.

The ability to differentiate between the two holds a clue to the practice and presence of the holy trinity as the highest argument for faith. If faith is not both an engagement and an experience, then it's little more than a good idea. If faith is not beautiful in its practice, then it can easily devolve into an argument and a polemic. And who is looking for another argument? Did Jesus die to win an argument? Did Jesus die to give us a better position paper?

One way to get a lock on this is to think outside the church for a moment.

The announcement of yet another good idea is an interesting thing to think about, but no more compelling than anyone else's interesting new idea. Even when the provenance is Jesus ("Jesus says" or "the Bible says"), it is not the inherent truth of the idea, but the beauty of expression and rarity of form ("Blessed are the poor in spirit...") that first wins a hearing. Later, the ultimate truth of faith will carry the day. But at first, it is the holy trinity of provenance, beauty, and rarity working together that captures attention.

BREWED FOR THOUGHT

What aspects and manifestations of the beauty of God drew you to God? What is it about God's beauty that keeps you coming back for more of God's presence?

Starbucks practices passion in order to perfect it, with the same expertise that it applies to coffee. If Christians hope to live with a grande passion, we need to perfect the three signature passions of the life of faith: the holy trinity of provenance, beauty, and rarity. When all three are present in our experiences, God is glorified and enjoyed.

LIFE'S FIRST AUTHENTIC PASSION: PROVENANCE

A better argument might batter your opponent into surrender, but it won't win anyone's heart. That's why the first element of authentic passion is provenance: the process of growing a soul that radiates such beauty that it bears the Maker's mark and bares the Creator's signature.

Most people today don't fret over whether Christianity can get them to heaven. They want to know: "Will it make me a better person?" Jesus did not call disciples so they could become Christlike. He called them so they could become "little Christs,"[3] or what I like to call spittin' images. Some linguists argue that the phrase *spittin' image* derives from the Southern dialect where *spirit* and *image* were contracted (some say corrupted) into one. To say that you are the spittin' image of your father is to say that you bear both his spirit and image. You bring together the visible and invisible, the tangible and the intangible, of your parent. Jesus enables us to be his spittin' image in both body and character. Like the lights above my dining-room table, the apprentice-made ones are Christlike, but the master-made one is Christ.

> *If you don't live it, it won't come out of your horn.*
>
> —JAZZ LEGEND
> CHARLIE "BIRD" PARKER[4]

The passion of Christian faith is the ability to say, "Yes, Christianity can make you a better person. That better person is Jesus." Christianity promises a provenance that can be certifiably Jesus. Authenticity is not about being more relevant but about being more Jesus. Do you speak with a Jesus voice? Do you see with Jesus eyes? Do you listen with Jesus ears? Do you touch with a Jesus touch?

The Experience and the Expression

Authentic Christian experience is not playing praise music on your car radio or placing your body in a pew to listen to a sermon. Authentic Christian

GROUNDS FOR TRUTH

At a conference in the mountains of North Carolina, Anglican writer Esther de Waal, a specialist in Celtic spirituality and monastic hospitality, asked two simple questions: Do people see Christ in us? Did we see Christ in them?[5] This is the question of spiritual provenance in shorthand.

experience is the process of establishing provenance, of growing into Christ. The world is not impressed that people attend church on Sunday morning. If anything, such a habit is viewed as a quaint waste of time. But imagine if every Christian in the world were living as a little Christ. Such provenance is not just a passionate transforming experience for the Christian; it's also a tantalizing expression of the gospel to the outside world. Starbucks opens stores on opposite street corners because of the draw of passion and authentic experience. But what is the draw of Christian faith if that faith is not practiced and experienced?

Early Christian mystics believed that God is born anew in every child. "Here comes God again," they would say, "in deep disguise." God wants to work the miracle of the Virgin Birth in every one of us. God wants to bring Jesus to life in every person and community. Just as the apple seed becomes the apple tree, and lemon seeds become lemons, so too, the seed of Christ in a human being can grow into a little Christ. The promise of the gospel is that Jesus can live his resurrection life in us. We were created for the communion of union with God.

GROUNDS FOR TRUTH

T. S. Eliot, one of the most influential poets of the twentieth century, liked to tell of a sign outside a baker's shop advertising bread for one dollar a loaf. You go into the shop, he said, hungry for bread and imagining the fresh smell of bread right out of the oven, only to find that inside the shop all that is for sale are copies of the sign advertising bread. Eliot suggested that the church was too much like that shop.[6]

Christianity pushes the experiential dimension of faith into more expressional forms of embodiment.[7] Rather than merely seeking experiences of

God, we are invited to become living expressions of God. Conversely, the repression of experience is the repression of expression. If we are not to end up like T. S. Eliot's Prufrock, measuring out our lives with coffee spoons,[8] experiences should lead us to become expressions. That same Holy Spirit who "brooded" over the chaos of the waters and brought creation to life broods over the chaos of our lives, bringing Christ to life in every one of us.

It follows that our expression becomes our confession. A confessional faith is where we end up: it's where an authentic expe-

> *Reason, that fool's gold for the bright.*
> —NOVELIST YANN MARTEL[9]

riential faith that has become expressional takes us.[10] True confessional Christianity is not propositional faith, but expressional faith. To know something, to communicate something, you have to become something. You have to establish provenance. The best things in life must be known firsthand, or not at all. Christians love truth like we love a person because Truth is a Person.[11]

Think and Drink

As I make a case for valuing experience far more highly than most of us have in the past, let me stress that the revenge of the right brain does not mean we can be anti-reason. I keep having to say it: God didn't put us through an Age of Reason for no reason. There are two kinds of men and women, it has been said: those who stop and think, and those who stop thinking. Inquisitions never have encouraged rational discussions of religious faith. Starbucks wants you to think as you drink, which is why they have started putting spiritually enriching quotes on their cups.

But your body is meant to do more than carry your head around. To bear the Creator's signature stamp of YHWH, you were designed by God to experience life with all your senses until you become an expression of the divine. For a God who threw the divine bodily into our midst, for a God who knows what it is to be human, divine provenance requires that spirituality not be divorced from materiality. A spirituality that does not bring together body and mind is like an unconsummated marriage. It's a spirituality that could well be annulled. Truth is discovered in the reciprocal worlds of thought, and embodied experiences and relationships. Authentic experiences of God are encoded in our bodies, which in turn encrypt our brains to better understand a God bigger than life, a God bigger than death.

I have an emotional connection with Starbucks. I have both a rational and an emotional connection with Christ. If anything, for Paul and the early church, rationalism presented as many problems if not more problems than mysticism.[12] Consider how much your life is governed by the Rationalist Posture: "It is wrong always, everywhere, and for anyone, to believe anything upon insufficient evidence"[13] versus the Faith Posture of the Bible: "Faith is the substance of things hoped for, the evidence of things not seen."[14]

Of course, our knowledge of the world is improperly shaped when we give either East or West a pass. Pope John Paul II liked to say that Christianity had been given two lungs, one Eastern and one Western, and that for too long the church has been breathing only out of her Western lung. For those of us who have burrowed into the rational furrow all our lives and learned to flex logical, linear muscles, all this talk about "emotional intelligence" and "feeling level" and "thinking-feeling" sends our unused lung coughing and wheezing. Even the greatest theologian of the Catholic church, Thomas Aquinas, admitted there is nothing in the mind that hasn't been put there by the senses.

> *The practice of philosophy and the attendance at philosophical schools seemed to the first Christians more of a disturbance than an opportunity.*
>
> —POPE JOHN PAUL II[15]

The Best Reason Is More Than Rational

The transition from rational to experiential is not a repudiation of the rational but a bonding of the emotional to the rational. It's like the bringing together of hydrogen and oxygen into H_2O. Or in phrasings with biblical resonance, "As [a man] thinks in his heart, so is he."[16] That thinking in the heart is the bonding of mind and heart into something less like a worldview and more like a worldstage.

Reason and emotion are reciprocal components to experience: if you reason that an experience will create something good, then you process that experience differently than if you think the experience will create something negative. To experience faith is to process what is received using the senses in both

> *Be not a baker if your head*
> *is made of butter.*
>
> —NINETEENTH-CENTURY SAYING

its "make sense" (thinking) and multisensory (fivefold) meanings. You can't truly experience something without thinking. If we can integrate the great traditions of the rational and the experiential, it will be a milestone for humanity. And think what it will do for your life of faith. Spiritual maturity comes when we learn when and how both to trust and mistrust experience.[17]

While we take bold action, we must subject our actions to the authority of the Christian community and to the Scriptures themselves,[18] which guard and guide our thoughts, feelings, and intuitions in walking and dwelling in the Truth.[19]

LIFE'S SECOND AUTHENTIC PASSION: BEAUTY

Life's second greatest passion is to grow a soul that is a beautiful work of art, a soul with such sensitivities that it can pick up signals of transcendence in the most unlikely of places, a soul with such stretch that it can experience the subtleties of life that separate the good from the bad, and the good from the great.

Granted, one must be careful about what one means by *beauty*. The nineteenth-century German philosopher Arthur Schopenhauer took this a little too far. He was once so offended by one man's looks that he attacked the man with his stick. One wonders what the philosopher might have done if on the street he had passed Jesus, who in the eyes of the world was without "form" and "comeliness" and without "beauty that we should desire him."[20]

While beauty signals the scent of the Spirit, beauty can also disguise the truth it is meant to display. Personal preference is one thing (and not grounds for attacking another), but uglification is another name for corruption. God created us as works of beauty. God created planet Earth as a masterwork of art. It is a sin to make ugly what God created beautiful. When you look at some real estate developments and see cookie-cutter monstrosities rubbing shoulders with one another, it takes all the strength one can muster not to get out Schopenhauer's cane and attack their developer.

BEAN THERE

If you think you're a coffee connoisseur, you've never met Ed Faubert. Faubert is a cupper who is certified by the New York Board of Trade. Put blindfolds on his eyes and a cup of coffee in his hands and he can tell from one sip "not just that it is from Guatemala, but from what state it comes, at what altitude it was grown, and on what mountain."[21]

In a world that creates traffic jams of experiences, Starbucks invites one to enter a world that is as rich in nuanced experiences and deep in distinctions as the *ampleur* of the Château Lafite Rothschild. In its "here try this," trial-and-success world of blends and drinks, Starbucks believes in the beauty of my experience and yours. They believe I can learn from and build on any experience I have, whether it's ghastly or marvelous. The romance of Starbucks coffee is precisely this: at Starbucks "we want to align ourselves with one of the greatest movements towards finding a connection with your soul."[22]

Starbucks is a business, and yet it understands the importance of the soul's need for experiences of beauty. But why are we so reluctant to grow a soul that takes deep breaths of beauty? Why are we so afraid to experience love that beats on the heart like a bass drum? And perhaps the most perplexing question of all: why are we so afraid to experience Christ or to let the beauty of Jesus be seen in us? In our bell-curve, mass-mind-set habits, too much of faith—even too much of God—is only vaguely remembered and not vividly experienced.

Christian faith is designed to be lived experiences of beauty, not well-structured thought experiments. In excavating the earliest church building on record, the third-century house church at Dura-Europas, archaeologists unearthed beautiful frescoes covering the walls in the room used for baptism, including one of Peter walking on the water with Jesus beckoning him forward. They also found children's drawings on the walls of what is thought to have been the teaching area.

Totally missing from the church today are the fossores, the professionals who dug the catacombs with picks and shovels and lamps, carved the inscriptions, decorated the graves, painted the walls, and presided at anniversary rituals.[23] Fossores were part artist, part architect, part laborer, part clergy, part gardener (keeper of the cemetery). The fossorian combination of three basic functions—laborer (ditch digger), artist (painter, sculptor, architect), and priest—speak to our ancestors' need for leaders proficient in the three transcendentals of being: beauty (create works of art), goodness (willingness to dig graves and carve stone slabs), and truth (ritual practices of formation and communion).

In the premodern world, the five senses were used to experience religious faith in various dimensions of beauty: the smell of burning incense and beeswax candles, the sound of bells big and small, the touch of a fingered rosary or *benetier,* the taste of the Eucharist or festival foods, the sight of tapestries and secret misericords, not to mention postures, gestures, ritual acts, mystery plays, passion plays, and town processions. In fact, all three Abrahamic religions are best understood in terms of beautifying one's relationship with God.

To see how far we have traveled down the rational path, look at your church. Don't focus on what it believes or its official statement of faith; rather, consider how much time your church expends in creating beauty. What does it do to develop embodied practices and multisensory experiences? For most of Christian history, the church was the major patron of the arts. But today, what role does art and poetry have in your worship? What works of art function as works of devotion in your spiritual life, enriching your home life and the life of your church?

Ugliness is life without design. "Designers are the new rock stars," trumpets a *Fast Company* cover headline.[24] Frank Gehry, Richard Meier, and Donna Karan are household names, and Michael Graves's thirty-dollar designer teapot at Target sits not all that far from designer sheets and designer toilet bowl brushes. When design reaches the level of toilet bowl brushes, it's time to take notice of a design revolution that is transforming every aspect of life.[25]

> *Art is a lie which makes us realize the truth.*
>
> —PABLO PICASSO

Dentists are now "smile designers,"[26] and cosmetic surgeons are "lifestyle artists" and "image consultants." Design is no longer optional or just an add-on. To qualify for a hearing, the church must convert to beauty and learn the narrative of aesthetics that constitutes the Grand Design. This is not a "designer spirituality,"[27] but a spirituality of Grand Design.

Religion is the real beauty business. But before we can live according to the passion of beauty, we have to understand what beauty is and isn't.

Beauty Is Not Pretty

Beauty is not movie-star pretty, a false beauty available only to consumers rich enough to pay for personal trainers and plastic surgeries. Prettiness is not beauty. Why is a Thomas Kinkade painting not beautiful, only pretty? Because it's a lie. There are no imperfections, no reality checks. It is afraid to tell the truth, afraid to do the hard work of beauty thinking and beauty living.

Why is the cross beautiful, but not pretty? Not because it's a vertical torture chamber, but because it tells the whole truth: the story of a God who loved us so much that God would go to well-curve extremes to show us that love. The cross is beautiful because it reveals love, the substance that bonds beauty, truth, and goodness together.

Why is Dove's campaignforrealbeauty.com such a huge success? Because it tells the truth: its television commercials feature real women with sizes closer to twelve than two, and with gray hair and crow's feet.[28]

Beauty Is Not Useful

When the Swiss biologist Adolf Portmann went ten miles down into the ocean depths, he found in the virgin darkness useless beauty—fish and other oceanic creatures festooned with complex designs and brilliant colors that no one could see or appreciate. No one except a God whose eyes hunger for beauty.[29]

Beauty Is Not Skin Deep; It Is Soul Deep

The connection between beautiful faces and beautiful souls often gets broken, as some people are so physically beautiful they don't feel the need to develop any personality. One of the reasons I love the island where I live is because it hasn't been discovered by "the beautiful people," who can be some of the ugliest people around.

Blemishes can be beauty spots. When you think of Marilyn Monroe, you think of her beauty spot: a real mole above her lip. When you think of Lauren Bacall, you think of her beauty spot: the space between her front teeth. Ditto Roger Moore's facial scar, Robert De Niro's multiple moles. Beauty is not a special-effects blender. Beauty is a soul bender. As blemished as we are, we all can be beauty spots for God.

Beauty Magnifies Message

You can tell someone "I love you" with words. Or you can say the same thing with flowers, which repeat "I love you" with smell, touch, and sight and say it for days, not seconds.

If not our churches, at least the homes we build and decorate are now beginning to integrate all five senses into their experience design. A home is not a home any longer unless there is sound (from indoor fountains to surround-sound stereo and sound of silence rooms), smell (home fragrances and aromatherapy), taste (killer kitchens as domestic solar plexus), touch (bed linens, throws, highly textured upholstery), and sight (including indoor courtyards and garden getaways, which offer up all five senses in one).[30] If in everyday life we want a home that adds to the rich experience of life, why do we remain so afraid to really experience our spiritual life?

GROUNDS FOR TRUTH

The English word *miracle* comes from the Latin words *miro* ("to wonder") and *mirus* ("wonderful"). It's the same root from which we get the word *mirror*. When you look in the mirror, do you wonder and admire the one-of-a-kind miracle you are? Or when you look in the mirror, do you see more copy than copyright? Jesus does not want look-alikes, only love-alikes.

LIFE'S THIRD AUTHENTIC PASSION: RARITY

My favorite sculptor (he was also an architect, painter, and poet), Gian Lorenzo Bernini (1598–1680), said art should create stupor in the beholder. The third member of the holy trinity of authenticity is rarity: a unique, one-of-a-kind creation with the provenance and beauty to create stupor in the beholder.

What prevents Christians from practicing that rarity of form that comes, not to those who join the crowd, but to those who make the crowd come to them: works of art as original and as diverse as Bob Dylan, Johnny Cash, Joni Mitchell, Tori Amos, Bono, T. D. Jakes, and Nelson Mandela, just to start the list? Community with God is never a mass, but a body, and in a body every member has a unique role and identity. In a mass there is duplication and replication, but not in a body, where every part is a miracle.

The One Thing That Makes God Sick

My Bible boasts a unique bookmark (details to come). It takes me quickly to the well-curve verse of the Bible and keeps me away from bell-curve temptations. In Revelation 3, God speaks to the church of Laodicea in language that translators have laundered, thereby proving the reason for God's warning in the first place.

"Would that you were hot or cold," God says, "but because you're lukewarm [or more precisely, play-it-safe, middle-of-the-road, mediocre], I'm going to spit [or spew, or in the best translation of the Greek, vomit] you out of my mouth."[31]

You didn't know there was a God-vomit verse in the Bible, did you? Above this verse I have written in the margins this paraphrase: "You make me sick, pew-potato church." That's why my bookmark is a Continental Airlines barf bag.

Whenever I want to join the crowd, or start to become faithful in my mediocrity: whenever I settle for growing a garden-variety soul, I get out my barf bag and remember that God loves variety that is vigorous and audacious. Rarity is a function of variety and passion: God made each one of us to be hot or cool, not tame or tepid. No wonder our ancestors used an oxymoron for passionate intensity: icy fire.[32] Shakespeare defined himself as "a man on fire for new words."[33] Jesus defined a disciple as a person on fire for God and the gospel, as someone born of water and of fire.[34] That's why our ancestors with this rarity of passion were often called *enthusiasts,* which comes from the Greek and means "God within." There is nothing that is halfhearted or halfway about a grande passion.

When Starbucks started its march to world coffee domination, they had a ten-second rule: anything that didn't get from the machine to your lips in ten seconds was thrown away and the barista started over. That's what it means to be hot about coffee. Most of the church literature I read tastes over-ripe and stale. Overripe and stale makes God sick.

One of my favorite gifts to pastors is a personalized vomit bag on which I write the abbreviated form of the warning this God-puke verse issues to every person and church: "Hot or Hurl." I then sign it "God." You can't have a love affair with lukewarm.

It makes me nauseatingly sick that half a dozen megachurches in USAmerica cast the molds for what goes on in the majority of Christian churches around the world. It's not their fault. It's ours. Time to get out the barf bag.

Theology of Barf Bags

One of my favorite sermons is to explore the theology of barf bags. For example, the Northwest Airlines barf bags read: "For Motion Sickness." A body not in motion is either paralyzed or dead. If you call yourself a church and can't handle change and mobility, if your church likes the stationary and loathes movement, time to get out the barf bag and hear these words booming from the heavens: "You make me sick, church."

The Continental Airlines barf bag reads on one side: "Seat Occupied." If your definition of following Jesus is occupying a seat for an hour a week, and then returning to business as usual,[35] it's time to hear these words: "You make me sick, church."

Risen from the dead, Jesus calls us to rise from the bed, stop occupying pews, and get preoccupied with participating in the resurrection life of Jesus. The church has more than enough mission statements and not nearly enough mission relationships and mission movements. Which brings us to our next chapter, an exploration of the Starbucks practice of participation—the second element in the EPIC life. But one more story before we go there.

A rough, uncultured man fell in love with a beautiful vase in a shop window. On the way to work he would stop and stare, transfixed by its shimmering colors and the dark red opaque radiance of the glass. When he summoned the courage to ask about the vase, he found that it was a rare, signed and dated, "Galle 1900" cameo vase. Very few Galle vases were made in this form of a red onion with its removable green stopper shaped like a leaf on a stem. The cost was equal to two months' salary, enough to take the man's breath away. But he arranged a layaway payment plan and in six months paid enough down that he could put the balance on his credit card.

When he brought the Galle home, he put it high on the mantel in his living room. There it sat, passing judgment on its surroundings. He had to keep the room clean to make it worthy of the vase. The grubby curtains needed to be replaced. The broken-down couch no longer seemed appropriate. The fluorescent light didn't bring out the colors of the Galle, so he purchased floor and table lamps. The room needed new wallpaper and re-painting. Gradually, his entire house was transformed.

Put the holy trinity of authentic passion on the mantel of your heart, and your whole life is transformed.[36]

Five

Life Is Empty
Until You Join In

ePic: Starbucks Is Participatory

You know you're drinking too much coffee when
you answer the door before people knock.

*A*n experience doesn't exist in a vacuum. It requires witnesses—otherwise who is around to verify that there was an experience to be had? And better (and more important) than witnesses, it demands participants. Authentic experiences, the ones that draw us in, insist that we join ourselves to the experience. An experience is compelling because it captures us and says, "Jump in."

If the gospel according to Starbucks teaches us anything, it is that sights, sounds, aromas, and flavors attract us. But attraction stops far short of satisfaction. What is a steaming cup of coffee that is left stranded on the counter?

Within minutes it is nothing but a cold, orphaned beverage. A cup of coffee isn't experienced and enjoyed until you participate with it. You don't go to Starbucks to look at coffee, to admire its deep hue, and to comment on its robust appearance. You go to Starbucks to drink it in, to participate in the experience of great coffee.

The same is true of spirituality, of course. You can read a book about prayer or worship. The words might inspire you, even challenge you. The ideas might intrigue you to the extent that you invest time in thinking about a particular spiritual discipline. But if you don't go ahead and pray or worship, the words written about these subjects are nothing more than dry ink. They are lifeless symbols of language that describe a spiritual experience that is impotent and useless until you choose to participate in it.

HOLY HALITOSIS?

Observing an experience might be inspiring, but meaning comes with your personal participation. Participating in what is before you makes it real.

And how do you know it's real? In the case of coffee, it's because you can smell it even after you've finished drinking it. The smell of those dark Brazilian beans can't be stifled even by "curiously strong" mints. Real experience leaves a scent on your breath that stays.

> *Fairy tales do not become beautiful until they are added to.*
>
> —TWENTIETH-CENTURY ITALIAN NOVELIST ITALO CALVINO[1]

The gospel is like that too. We can mass-produce an instant, crystallized version that we keep in the freezer. It's tasteless and unobtrusive, completely harmless and always convenient. Or we can plunge into a strong, heady, aromatic experience that leaves us forever changed—down to our very odor. That's the experience of the gospel.

GRANDE PASSION IS PARTICIPATORY

I dare you to try something. Go into any Starbucks, stand at the counter, and say these words: "A cup of coffee, please." Watch what happens next.

The whole place comes to a screeching halt. No one knows how to deal with you. You have thrown the ultimate monkey wrench into the inner workings of the system. Your monkey wrench is also a money wrench because thinking of Starbucks as a place to get a cup of coffee would be disastrous to their bottom line.

BREWED FOR THOUGHT

What is your favorite flavor combination when it comes to coffee-related beverages? Have you ever gone into a specialty coffee shop and ordered a simple cup of coffee? What happened? Can you make up your own slang for a coffee drink (for example, "heaven on the lips but nothing on the hips")?

Now try ordering again. This time, ask for my signature drink: a double-tall skim latte extra hot. Place the order and watch what happens next. The whole place lights up. Suddenly everyone and everything starts humming with activity. Your cup is personalized, its six boxes tattooed with your peculiar preferences.

If I've had too many double-tall skim lattes extra hot, I order a double-tall skim decaf latte extra hot, which often earns a smile and a snide comment, "This guy wants a 'Why bother?'" Oh, for the simplicity on the other side of complexity.

Learning to Speak Starbucks

I shall never forget an order I placed at a Columbus (Ohio) Starbucks, across the street from Trinity Lutheran Seminary where I was lecturing. The experience is etched in my memory for two reasons. One, the Starbucks store was in an old bank building, so you could take your venti frappuccino into the vault and drink it there. Second, my exchange with the barista is one that is still with me as if it happened yesterday.

I love the fact that Starbucks is open at an early and dark hour of 5:30 a.m. My early-and-dark drink is a "black eye." My friend Steve Laue says that having your favorite brew waiting for you at the cash register is like having your own pew in church. But in Columbus, Ohio, when I asked for a black eye, my order was thrown back at me: "You know, sir, that's not in the book."

"But you know what it is, right?"

"Yeah, I know what it is. But it's not in the book."

"Is a 'red eye' in the book?"

"No, that's not in the book either."

"But you know what a red eye is, right?"

"It's not in the book, sir."

"Okay," I said. "I give up. What book are you talking about?"

"The Starbucks Book, our bible," he said, as he handed me a little cream-colored booklet entitled "Make It Your Drink." When I opened it, the first page leaped into my face even more than the Starbucks employee had. In big letters it read, "Learning the Lingo."

This was not a training manual written for aspiring baristas. This was a booklet designed to be read by customers. Starbucks expects us to learn its lingo. Members of its staff are trained to help us comprehend a language we do not yet speak. Starbucks doesn't say, "I won't serve you until you learn my lingo." But it does want us to learn its tribal lingo and offers resources such as this catechesis to help tutor us. *So much for the seeker-sensitive coffee shop,* I thought. And what does it say for the seeker-sensitive church?

Starbucks wants us to participate fully in the experience, even to the extent of learning to speak a new language. Talk about being immersed in coffee culture. Of course, Starbucks would like you to try as many drinks as possible as you learn its lingo, and the "Make It Your Drink" booklet is designed to help you mix and match as you perfect your signature drink. There are fifty-five thousand possible drink combinations on the board at a typical Starbucks.

Sure enough, as I flipped through the booklet I couldn't find a black eye. But here was a new dialect, a living language growing from the ground up. I then thought of how differently I would order my early-and-dark drink if I were at a Caribou Coffee in either Atlanta or Minneapolis. At Caribou Coffee I wouldn't order a black eye (coffee of the day with two shots of espresso; a red eye adds one shot of espresso). At Caribou, I'd order "two shots in the dark." At Dunkin' Donuts, I'd order a "Turbo Hot." And if I were ordering at the most righteous, right-on, politically correct coffeehouse, Peet's of Berkeley, I'd order "two depth charges."

Suddenly it hit me: I'm multilingual in coffee. Is that sick or what?

If we can be multilingual in coffee, why not in other areas of life? Is there only one way to say, "I'm a Christian" or "Do you know God?" If I am talking to someone who is not immersed in the evangelical world, how can I communicate if I speak only one dialect, the in-house lexicon of formal religion?

INNOVATION THROUGH PARTICIPATION

In the postmodern world, "custom" is returning to the customer. At Jones Soda Co., which is now a partner with Starbucks (and Target), almost everything about a Jones Soda is designed by the customer. They will even create custom-made labels so that it's literally your soda for $34.95 a twelve-pack.[2] Other companies such as Lego, Kettle Foods, and John Fluevog shoes encourage customers to create their own flavors, styles, and products. You can even customize postage and print your own stamps with personal photos and logos in Australia, Canada, Switzerland, Singapore, Hong Kong, China, Taiwan, Indonesia, the Netherlands, and finally in USAmerica.[3] You can see the same participatory thrust in license plates, cell phone ring tones, creative haircuts, and what some might call the unlikely revival of liturgy in religion. In a way, it's as if the Jesus Movement of the 1960s and 1970s cleared the cultural palate so the boomers' Gen-X children could reapproach liturgy and sacramental tradition without the modern social baggage that had numbed their parents.

In the past, companies resisted customer innovation in favor of highly paid researchers and costly R&D departments. Today, though, new products are developed for little or nothing through DIY (do it yourself) innovation, drawing on lead users or "luminaries." Called user-led innovation, this approach gladly consults customers on how to reinvent and improve products as diverse as scientific instruments, sports equipment, construction materials, and coffee. In fact, one corporate insider contends that "the majority of innovation" now happens through co-creation with customers.[5] A huge benefit is that customers are more prone to design products not for final use but for evolvability, which enables future modifications and extensions.

> *Organizations dominated by control, compliance, and compartmentalization (the three C's) are being outpaced by organizations that focus on ideas, information, and interaction (the three I's).*
>
> —MANAGEMENT GURU
> MANFRED KETS DE VRIES[4]

This does not mean that the customer is always right. To think that is for a company to lose its soul. But the customer must participate for a product to be right.

WEB 2.0: POWER TO THE PEOPLE

I could stand in line at Starbucks from morning dark to midnight and never taste a drop of coffee. Standing in line isn't what makes going to Starbucks worth the trip. To get what's worth the price of admission, you have to place an order (in whatever dialect connects), and then drink the beverage. What makes the Starbucks experience work is your participation. Without it, you're just standing there—and you might as well stand somewhere else if you're not going to participate. The money I pay for a latte is a kind of entrance fee exacted for participation in the Starbucks experience.

When I walk into a Starbucks, the more I participate, the more positively experiential it becomes. The art of a Starbucks experience is not performance art, but participation art. Starbucks has bet its future on the fact that future culture is not reactive, but interactive. While our educational systems still reward linear thinking and passive learning, digital culture rewards lateral thinking as well as role playing and other forms of participation.[6] People need to participate in the production of content, whether it is coffee, college degrees, music, ice cream, or classified ads.

The distinction between consumer and producer, server and served, professional and amateur, is fading fast. Starbucks doesn't have employees but "partners" where everyone gets a green apron. Coffee Masters are given black aprons, and every partner is encouraged to aspire to being one of these Jedi Mas-

> *When it comes to traditional media, teen girls today want it interactive and responsive. The most popular features at Channel One are interactive—things that allow girls to express their own voice and influence an outcome.*
>
> —MORGAN WANDELL, executive VP, Channel One[7]

ters of Coffee. The Starbucks experience heralds a new era of connection between customers, employees, and shareholders. Everyone participates, which invests the experience with a level of interest and meaning that keeps everyone engaged.

In fact, audience participation may well be the twenty-first century's golden calf. You can find this new architecture of participation all over the Web: user-generated content, blogs, social networking, to name only a few. Al Gore's cable television venture, Current TV, aims to be almost entirely viewer-produced, where "VC²" now means "viewer-contributed content."[8] Converse Gallery is a Web site where enthusiasts sent in twenty-four-second films inspired by the popular sneakers. The best became Converse's television ads.[9]

The magic of the iPod, the signature technology of our era, is not its pack-of-cards size. It is its promise of a lifetime play list, a soundtrack of the soul that every person, now a DJ (and soon a VJ), produces herself. The iPod delivers a death blow to all silver platters because nothing else comes close to being as interactive.[10] When focus groups are now being used at all, they are designing products, not evaluating and judging products already on the market. Choice is not a choice any longer. It's mandatory.

> *Digital technology, abetted by the Internet, is turning fans from passive acolytes to active participants in the artistic process.*
>
> —MATTHEW MIRAPAUL[11]

Flying Pigeon Bicycle Co. was China's biggest bike builder in the 1970s and early '80s, when there was a multiyear waiting list to get its forty-five-pound black one-speeds. In 1986, it sold more than three million bikes. But in the late 1980s and '90s, other bike companies started offering more colors than black. These companies also started producing racing bikes, mountain bikes, and road bikes.

Flying Pigeon kept to its success: black one-speeds. In 1998, the company sold two hundred thousand bikes. By 2004, Flying Pigeon was flying again. They are now selling more than one million bikes. Why? Flying Pigeons now come in three hundred models and dozens of colors. In spite of Mao's dictum that all every Chinese person needed was roof, rice, and a bike, the era of basic black or a "Mao bike" is gone.[12]

OUR KARAOKE CULTURE AND WIKI FUTURE

One of the greatest cultural shifts occurring on a global scale is the wikification of all aspects of life, which is fueling the social movement from representation to participation. Wiki is a kind of open-source server software that enables users to create and edit Web pages using any Web browser. It encourages democratization and decentralization and deprofessionalization, as anyone is free to shape the content without any controls other than the community that monitors the contributions. This wikification, or open-sourcing, of human existence started long before the Web.

Think about the end of the Cold War. It wasn't a military victory or a political triumph. It was rather the competition between the processes of market-driven versus centrally planned economic systems. But the Internet is fueling and refueling this massive shift away from representative democracy toward more participatory democracy, a shift that is transforming everything from politics to economics to religion and the arts.

But before we take a brief look at what is happening in the political arenas, let's look at two areas most immediately being redefined by the cultural transfer from representation to participation: television "watching" (rise of reality shows) and "spectator" sports (growth of extreme sports).[13]

REALITY TV AT ITS BEST

The P in EPIC is redefining how everything on television is presented, from the news to fund-raisers[14] to prime-time programming.

In the first week of February 2006, USAmericans had a choice: to watch celebrities perform their best music on the 2006 Grammy Awards Show, or to watch wannabe celebrities in hotel basements audition for spots on *American Idol*. Guess which program they picked? The amateurs were more attractive by more than ten million viewers.[15] NBC paid enormous sums of money to broadcast the 2006 Winter Olympics. The second week of February there was this network face-off: either watch the Fox talent show *American Idol* or NBC's 2006 Winter Olympics. Guess which show won?[16]

BEAN THERE

Artist Dale Johnson has elevated the mural from lone creation to community event. His form of participation art he calls neighborhood art. Johnson paints scenes of neighborhood people and landscapes on the sides of buildings. In the process of implementing his art he gets people from the neighborhood to help him paint. As mural art is created, new forms of relationships and community also come into being.

American Idol is the first show in USAmerica run by the television audience. The 1950s' hits *Queen for a Day* (Jack Bailey) and *This Is Your Life* (Ralph Edwards) were the first quasi-reality television shows, but it was the studio audiences that chose the queen or featured the life. The success of *American Idol* shows that we have gone from watching people become stars to choosing tomorrow's stars ourselves and needing to feel involved in their climb and claw toward stardom.[17]

Megastardom and solo performers are not social necessities, but social constructions. And these constructions are being dismantled in favor of a well-curved phenomenon of celebrity culture fashioned from the ground up on the one end, and everyone-a-celebrity (and for more than fifteen minutes) on the other.

Most surprising of all about the other end of celebrity culture, once we pick our stars, we are loyal to them. Look at the record sales for the winners of *American Idol,* and even the fortunes that accrue to the also-rans. Runner-up Clay Aiken was so popular that his school had to have a private, tickets-only graduation ceremony for his commencement in North Carolina.[18]

Most surprising of all about the other end of everyone-a-celebrity is the global distribution of one's artistry without recording companies or other forms of commercial mediation. In premodern cultures, everyone sang and danced. Everyone made music. Everyone made art. In the modern world, fewer and fewer people actually made music or art.[19] Technological evolution is now enabling people to become musicians and artists and to be able to distribute their music and art.

BEAN THERE

The Travel Channel struggled to find the winning formula until it introduced one little EPIC element that made the *World Poker Tour* a huge success and the channel's highest-ranking program. What made all the difference between success and failure? The strategic placement of cameras so that viewers can see each player's hand: reality TV at its best.

In 2000, more USAmericans watched the *Survivor* finale than voted for George W. Bush or Al Gore. In 2000, 105 million votes were cast in the presidential election. In 2002, one hundred million total votes were cast in the first *American Idol* competition.[20] You say, "But those voters often cast multiple votes." I say, "Well, have you ever heard of Florida, the home of my favorite postmodern bumper-sticker: 'Don't blame me. I voted for both of them.'"

Reality TV has nothing to do with reality, but everything to do with making television into an interactive medium. By itself, television is a passive medium.[21] It creates couch potatoes; it creates pew potatoes and "seeker worship." The Internet is an interactive medium and creates people who can't just sit there but need to participate.[22] Reality TV is transforming television from a paradigm of performance to a paradigm of participation.[23]

EXTREME SPORTS: MY HERO STEVE BARTMAN

Years ago in a comedy routine, Bill Cosby told about dating a philosophy major at Temple University. She was interested in such questions as "Why is there air?" As an athlete and physical education student, Cosby knew the answer: "To fill basketballs."

Today the air is leaking out of basketballs, footballs, baseballs, soccer balls, and tennis balls, to name but a few. One story tells why. The year was 2003. It was game six of the National League Championship Series. The Chicago Cubs were one inning away from breaking the curse of missing the World Series for the fifty-seventh consecutive season. That is, until Steve Bartman came into play. Steve Bartman was then a twenty-six-year-old Cubs fan who knew the game inside and out and coached a youth baseball team. His greatest dream was for the Cubs to play the Boston Red Sox in the World Series.

But Bartman was raised in a karaoke culture where the hardest thing to do is to just sit there. So when the Marlins batter slammed the ball to where Bartman was seated in left field, he couldn't just sit still and watch the batter hit a home run. He had to catch the ball and put the batter out. So he lunged for the ball and interfered with left fielder Moises Alou, who in the tussle with Bartman dropped the ball.

Alou threw a hissy fit. The city of Chicago threw a hissy fit. A police guard had to be posted outside the Northbrook, Illinois, home where Bartman lived. Media helicopters hovered over his home, hoping to catch an image of the guy who "cost the Cubs the World Series." It got so bad that Bartman contemplated taking the advice of some columnists who recommended that he move to Miami.

What Cubs manager Dusty Baker should have done was to bring Bartman with him into the dugout for game seven of the championship series to celebrate the Cubs' number one fan. Because the future is more Steve Bartman than Moises Alou, more interactive than passive, more about people creating their own experiences as forms of self-expression than passively observing someone else's experience. Kids no longer want to watch. They now can be their own stars, not like Mike but Mike himself, not like Moises Alou but Alou himself.

The inability of professional sports to grasp this karaoke culture assures it a problematic future. If Steve Bartman wasn't a sufficient wake-up call, perhaps they need to look up at the fans wearing painted faces, waving original signs, and chanting home-made cheers. For the same reason kids don't go to

BREWED FOR THOUGHT

Feel free to try this at home: ask any fifteen-year-old whether sports video games or sports TV will be more popular in the future. When teenagers want reality, they don't go to a game and watch, they play the real game. There is a fortune waiting to be made by someone who will invent an EPIC sport: a sport where the boundaries between athlete and spectator are broken down, and where the interaction of the crowd can actually shape the outcome of the game. Why couldn't a leaping catch by Steve Bartman in the stands put out the batter? (Sadly, the Romans got it right the wrong way—they had such a game. It involved Christians and lions.)

concerts to sit there (they go to dance and mosh and hold lighters in the air), if spectators can't become part of the show in some way, they won't go.

As I'm writing this, I have a fifteen-year-old son and a ten-year-old daughter. Getting my son to go to a Seattle Mariners game is almost as hard as getting him to go to the dentist. I keep telling him that baseball is an extreme sport—it's so slow it's a sports sabbatical. My daughter thinks the "sport" of tennis is a joke like I used to think NASCAR was a joke. But from an EPIC standpoint, she wins the argument. In tennis, you have players who will not hit a little ball over a net until there is complete silence: in other words, total nonparticipation of the fans or coaches. No life is on the line in tennis.

Not so with NASCAR, whose cars are filled with cameras and microphones so people in the stands, in the parking lots, and at home on the Web can feel as if they are parts of the pit crew or passengers in the cars. And in every race, lives are on the line. Tennis's pathetic attempt to increase the level of participation is to promise that three times during a match the player will hit a ball into the stands for someone to catch. The fact that Roger Federer is perhaps the greatest tennis player in history and does not have superstar status with my son or daughter (or with their friends) suggests that the future of tennis is cricket.

With the exception of the NFL, all the major professional sports are in decline. Every professional golfer ought to thank God daily for Tiger Woods, for his celebrity star status is the only thing keeping their sport in the media spotlight and them in the money stream. The financial health of the NFL is mainly due to media contracts and billion-dollar licensing agreements with video-game companies.[24] Even though the NFL rakes in the dough from television contracts, few analysts will argue that networks make money on the sport. What Sunday afternoon football represents is the last major mass market…the last mass audience for network television in a world of iPod, cable, wireless devices, satellite radio, PlayStation, and Xbox.[25]

While mainstream sports are being abandoned, especially by younger males,[26] extreme sports are becoming the new mainstream. The fastest-growing sports are skateboarding and snowboarding. By 2001, more kids were buying skateboards than baseball gloves.[27] Ron Semiao, who helped create the X Games, calls skate parks the ball fields of the twenty-first century.

Only two things are keeping professional sports going for postmoderns: fantasy sports,[28] and video games. Both put EPIC handles on professional athletics, enabling postmoderns to pick it up.

John Madden is one of the most recognizable names in professional sports and a 2006 inductee into the Football Hall of Fame. The statistical measure of pop culture clout is called the Q Score. Madden's Q Score is in the top ten of all sports and higher than any current football player. He is instantly recognizable by younger kids, who come up to him and say, "Hey, Madden!"

If they call him by his last name only, it's a video game connection. The Madden series of NFL games has sold more than forty-three million copies since 1989. We still haven't comprehended the significance of this one figure: the video game industry is about twice the size of the Hollywood industry.

> ...that as video games got so graphically close to perfection, and you could create your own players...that there might be a battle between seeing games in person or on television and seeing it play out on a video game.
>
> —NBA COMMISSIONER DAVID STERN, when asked, "What's your worst fear?"[29]

DIRECT DEMOCRACY

Gutenberg made everybody a reader. Xerox made everybody a publisher. Interactive telecommunications is making everybody a lobbyist and politician. Interactivity is no longer an add-on or plug-in; it is becoming the centerpiece of all we do, the fulcrum of the future.

There are two key ideas in the European Constitution: *civil society* and *participatory democracy*. The link between *participatory* and *democracy* varies from country to country, but what all share in common is a demand for new forms of political participation that go far beyond simply being allowed to cheer for professional politicians from the sidelines or one chance to register a preference every four years.[30] By combining representative government (in which elected leaders actually make the key decisions) with direct democracy (in which the general public and blogosphere play central roles in the decision-making process), a new form of deliberative democracy is emerging. People are replacing the press, literally being the fourth branch of the government. The move from representation to participation can also be seen in Oregon's all mail-in ballot, eliminating voting booths. With an ethic of participation rather than representation, it is inevitable that mail-in ballots themselves will be replaced by digital balloting.

But the phenomenon of participation is more than political. It is universal. Edwin Schlossberg is called the grand master of interactivity. After receiving a PhD in literature and science at Columbia, he worked with Buckminster

BEAN THERE

"Early in the 1988 presidential election campaign, when the democratic nominee, Massachusetts Governor Michael Dukakis, actually was leading Vice President Bush in the polls, my granddaughter Sarah happened to be watching the nightly news with her parents. Sarah heard Tom Brokaw report the findings of the latest NBC News/*Wall Street Journal* poll. 'Vice President George Bush is closing the gap,' Brokaw announced. Sarah turned to her parents in tears. 'I love that store,' she wailed. 'Why would he want to close the Gap?' "[31]

Fuller and installed his first interactive design in 1977 when he developed exhibits for the Brooklyn Children's Museum. His New York City design company, ESI, was founded that same year. Schlossberg makes his living designing interactive experiences, completing in 2002 the twenty-million-dollar New York Times Square interactive sign for Reuters, a global information company.

In 1998 Schlossberg published a book titled *Interactive Excellence* in which he argues that excellence is now a collaborative process involving both speaker and audience.[32] In fact, he continues, standards of excellence can be raised by increasing the interaction on every front. Schlossberg ends the book with this stunning sentence: "Excellence exists only in the variety and quality of our interactions."[33]

Schlossberg is not anti-performance. In fact, everything that was performance is now becoming a participation art. Notice in what direction the pop star points the mike. Note who is being spotlighted.[34] Hillsongs songwriter/worship leader Darlene Zschech transitions to lead worshiper when she hands the song over to the congregation and hangs her head in silent worship. P.O.D. lead singer Sonny Sandoval, known as much for his waist-length dreadlocks as for his spiritually minded hard rock, often tosses the microphone into the audience and lets the crowd take over while he remains onstage, mouthing the words with no mike.[35]

Starbucks is a karaoke culture. And it's getting more karaoke with every passing frappuccino. The essence of a karaoke culture is not that you have to hold the mike or that "I have to get my own way" (which is more control than participation). The essence of karaoke is that the mike is there to pick up if you really want to. But most of the time I'm content to enjoy and participate in others' participations.

By the way, I did finally get my early-and-dark black eye. But only after a couple more rounds of, "Yes, I know I'm ordering something that isn't in the book… Yes, I know it's not in the book… Okay, okay, it's not in the book."

There are fundamentalists everywhere.

Six

The Gospel
in a Participatory Cup

Get Fully Immersed in What God Is Doing

Jesus took bread, gave thanks and broke it,
and gave it to his disciples, saying,
"Take and eat; this is my body."
—MATTHEW 26:26

An old General Electric commercial became one of the most successful advertising campaigns in history. The appeal was captured in just six words: "We Bring Good Things to Life."

If Jesus launched an advertising campaign, he might use this slogan: "I Bring Things Good, True, and Beautiful to Life."

The Incarnation—God taking on human flesh—is a participatory event. But we have made it representational. God did not send a representative to earth. Neither did God dispatch some prophetic plenipotentiary to have a meeting with us. God sent "very God of very God" to be one of us. Even in the Incarnation, God invites participation; Mary had to say yes: "May it be to me as you have said." Jesus was God in the flesh, summoning us to be sent and spent in mission in the world, in partnership with our Creator.[1] We are participants in Jesus' resurrection life and partners in creation. We, too, bring things to life by participating in the divine life.

FROM GREAT TO G.O.O.D.

This is what *missional* means: to participate in the mission of Jesus in the world, to incarnate in the experiences of our lives and our communities the good news of God's love for the world. We must become a G.O.O.D. Church, which stands for Get Out Of Doors. We must get out of the church building and venture into the world to join the God who fills a "the hungry with good things."[2]

We Bring True Things to Life.

We Bring Beautiful Things to Life.

We Bring Good Things to Life.

When celebrity architect Frank Gehry insists on a participatory, collaborative methodology in his creations,[3] he is taking a cue from his Creator, who built into the universe a participationist structure to divine creation and human creating. In fact, the church's greatest teacher, Thomas Aquinas, defined human *esse* as "participation in divine *esse*." In other words, the essence of a human being is participation in the essence of the divine being.

For premodern Christian thinkers such as Aquinas, as well as Augustine or Anselm, *reason (logos)* was understood and experienced less as mental thought and more as something "radically participant in the divine and the cosmos."[4] To be created in the image of God, to live *imago Dei*, is to participate in the divine life and the divine creativity. God the Architect compels an architecture of participation for the Spirit's ongoing architecture of creation, re-creation, and final creation.

I have a randomizing restaurant ritual that turns eating in a strange restaurant from an activity into an EPIC-tivity. When the server brings me the menu, I ask his or her name (if the server is not wearing a name tag) and then ask two questions: "What is this restaurant known for?" That question usually gets a quick response. Then comes my second question: "Now tell me: what is your favorite item on the menu?"

Brewed for Thought

Read this sentence again: the essence of a human being is participation in the essence of the divine being. Think about what Thomas Aquinas's teaching means to you and for you. In what ways do you participate in the life of God? In what ways does this participation define your essence as a person?

The first question is a setup for the second. If the response is, "Oh, it's all good. Everything on the menu is good," I know I'm in trouble. Ditto, "I'm a vegetarian, so I don't eat here." But if I receive a passionate response as to why the server likes a certain item, and I order that item, I'm in for a delightful experience. My waiter has an investment in my liking that entrée and will do everything possible to make good on that recommendation.

Of course, inviting this type of participation involves certain risks. Sometimes I eat food that doesn't belong on any diet. The Republican National Committee had to shut down its Make Your Own Campaign Poster Web site when large numbers of detractors mocked the Bush/Cheney ticket in 2004. The *Los Angeles Times* tried to involve readers in the writing of editorials,

Wikipedia style. But they had to suspend the experiment because people posted obscene photos on the site.[5] Despite the risks, there are even greater risks in nonparticipation, in not tapping into the collective intelligence of people and the Web-brain.

People long to participate. The worst thing you can say about a worship service is that it is uninvolving. Worship wars in churches are better described as EPIC wars, since the battle is less about the type of music than it is about the degree of participation. Liturgical music composer Marty Haugen likes to tell the story of the church organist who complained, "No matter how loud I play I can still hear the people singing."[6]

In EPIC worship the congregation is not a passive consumer of content, but a participant in the creation and refinement of the experience. For example, increasingly the congregation is part of the act of sermon composition and design. In the future it will be less the dynamics of human absorption than the dynamics of human interaction that shape the homiletic form. Quality is raised by increasing the interaction on every front, especially between the preacher and the congregation. In the modern world of pulpit-centric preaching, great effort was spent on how to write better opening sentences. In EPIC preaching, time is spent on how to create better opening (and closing) interactions.

My favorite way of EPIC preaching is to work with a live Web-feed and a VJ. I call this VJ (preferably a teenager who grew up on Google) my dancing partner. I stand in the middle of the congregation, with my print Bible open to a text that is also featured on one of the screens up front. Together the congregation and I exegete the leading image(s) of the text. A second screen, however, displays images that are under the creative promptings of my dancing partner. While the congregation and I immerse ourselves in the Word, my dancing partner is Googling the Web for images that are tossed up by our interactions. These images are displayed on the second screen as contributions to and animations of our conversation. The energy that flows from these multilayered connections cannot be described.

That said, not everyone will get it. In the mid-1990s I preached what some are calling the first Web-based sermon with a live (but very slow) Web-feed. It took place at the Kentucky

> *We are called to participate with the Lord of history in the creation of history.*
> —COMPOSER/CONDUCTOR
> THOMAS HOHSTADT

Pastors' School for the United Methodist Church. When the organizers sent me the written evaluations, I was drawn to one in particular. The pastor had stated: "Sweet was a total waste of time. Left the pulpit and tried to talk to us while using the Internet. Got nothing out of it."

There can be a disconnect between longing to participate and actually getting involved. People want to participate in an organic way, not in a strategic or formulaic way. They are not interested in our strategies of participation; they are interested in the participation itself. Authentic participation is a fusion of two components, best captured in words you don't often hear in casual conversation: spizzerinctum and sprezzatura.

SPIZZERINCTUM: HOLY BOLDNESS

Authentic participation requires what in Appalachian culture is often called a good shot of spizzerinctum. Nothing gets accomplished without spizzerinctum, a word that combines initiative, industry, independence, and spontaneity. Perhaps the closest synonym is *chutzpah* ("holy boldness"), but chutzpah with responsibility, hospitality, and the will to succeed.

Jesus operates with spizzerinctum. His love is daring, imaginative, bold, and in the moment. It catches you off guard and sometimes comes off looking unfair and unpredictable. But life is unfair and unpredictable. The gospel

of Jesus never promises us comfort. When did Jesus get treated fairly? Fair is
a fairy tale (and not a very exciting one).

BREWED FOR THOUGHT

How many Christians do you know whose lives demonstrate
holy boldness? What does that quality look like?

Harold Macmillan, prime minister of Britain from 1957–63, gave a quick
response to the question of what most threatened to derail a prime minister's
plans and platform: "Events, dear boy, events!"[7] The only absolute certainty
of your life and mine is one we don't like to talk about: death. Everything else
is a gift and a grab bag.

Participating in the mission of Jesus requires massive shots of spizzerinctum: "For God has not given us a spirit of cowardice,"[8] but of holy boldness.
John Bunyan, best known for *The Pilgrim's Progress,* is the source of this
phrase "holy boldness." In a little-known treatise, Bunyan writes:

> Living by Faith, begets in the Heart a Son-like Boldness and Confi-
> dence to God-ward, in all our Gospel-Duties; under all our Weak-
> nesses, and under all our Temptations. It is a blessed thing to be
> privileged with an holy Boldness and Confidence God-ward, that
> he is on our side, that he taketh part with us, and that he will plead
> our Cause with them that rise up against us.[9]

The Death of Spontaneity

Typical Christians are much more at home in the plan than in the moment,
more at ease following someone else's formula than making it up as we go
along. But spizzerinctum involves the habit of saying yes to the moment.

Jesus received each moment as a gift, less going after what he wanted than wanting what came to him.

His speech reflected the same approach to life. In a content analysis of the one hundred twenty-five incidents of Jesus' encounters with people, Ralph L. Lewis has found that "roughly 54 percent of those encounters are initiated by His hearers. Instead of standing up and proclaiming the message He wanted the people to hear, He responded to His audience's questions, objects, doubts. He allowed and welcomed their involvement."[10]

My favorite spontaneity story has to do with the recording of what *Rolling Stone* magazine called "the greatest song of all time"[11]—Bob Dylan's "Like a Rolling Stone" (1965), with its trademark Hammond organ background. Guitarist Al Kooper, known for organizing Blood, Sweat & Tears and discovering Lynyrd Skynyrd, showed up hoping to play guitar for the recording session. Banished to the production booth by the superior skills of guitarist Michael Bloomfield, Kooper would not be sidelined. He wanted in on the action, so he sneaked back into the studio and slid quietly into the vacant organ bench. When Dylan began recording the song, Kooper threw into the mix of sounds some organ chords that he made up on the spot. If you listen carefully, you will note how these chords are stutter-stepped into the sound. That's because Kooper didn't really know how to play the organ, and wasn't sure what chords he was playing until he heard them.

When the producer realized what Kooper was up to, he ordered him back to the sound booth. But Dylan was in the moment. For him the recording of the song was more free play than planned execution. He heard a rare sound being born with the mix of cymbals, organ, and guitar. And he famously shouted over the confusion a shot of spizzerinctum: "Turn the organ up."[12]

Participation turns the spontaneity up. Part of our problem is we have an image of God as The Grand Master of Chess Moves, moving players around on the board of life, able to checkmate at any moment and end the game. It is easier for us to think of Jesus as Monologue than as Conversation Partner.

But Jesus was not premeditated in his approach to life. In fact, he was the most spontaneous person who ever lived.

As a boy when he was learning in the temple, he decided on the spot to stay longer than expected and threw a monkey wrench in his parents' plans. His spizzerinctum shocked even his parents. Similarly, Jesus did not draw up careful job descriptions for the Twelve. Rather, while wandering the country-side (even in his lifetime travel radius of thirty-five miles Jesus took unpredictable arcs), he decided one day that it was time to put together a team. Seeing some fishermen on the shore, he stopped and said with holy boldness, "You'll do. Follow me."

That took spizzerinctum.

BREWED FOR THOUGHT

Do you spend more time dreaming or planning? Think about your life in light of carefully made plans. How much confidence do you place in your plans? Do you find security and comfort in carefully thought-out plans? And even when you have set forth elaborate plans in advance, how many times have you accomplished exactly what you planned?

Any reading of the gospels reveals a Jesus not needing to be in control. Instead, we see a Jesus who is open to being surprised by life and responding spontaneously to the circumstances around him.[13] Jesus was free-flowing music, not formulaic math. He didn't pencil people into his crowded schedule. Rather, he lived in the immediacy of the moment and fell in love with whomever he met, whether it was a rich young ruler who had everything or a little man in a tree.[14]

That took spizzerinctum.

How many times did Jesus heal people using exactly the same words, questions, and actions? He did not mobilize a strategic healing plan for the blind, lame, and paralyzed waiting at the pool of Bethesda. He did not heal every sick individual lying around the pool. He picked one out from the crowd and cured him of his thirty-eight-year paralysis. Jesus healed each person in a way, and at a time and place, appropriate to each.

That took spizzerinctum.

Spontaneity Goes Deep[15]

Eastern cultures have a lot to teach us about hospitality. We've come to think of hospitality as having people over for dinner, or the hospitality industry. But hospitality is more about the treatment of strangers than friends or guests. How often do we treat strangers with as much care as we show a guest? How often do we show that level of care to an enemy? In the movie *House of Sand and Fog*, an Iranian (Ben Kingsley) and his wife welcome into their home a woman who was hurt. They take care of her even though she is actively trying to take their home away from them.[16]

That takes spizzerinctum.

It was because of his deep spontaneity that Franciscan priest Maximilian Kolbe is remembered today throughout the world as "The Man for Others." In the summer of 1941 a prisoner escaped from Kolbe's cell block at Auschwitz. Standard procedure in cases of escape was to punish the entire cell block involved by randomly selecting ten prisoners and either lining them up to be shot in front of everyone or sending them to an underground bunker to be starved, tortured, and executed. When Father Kolbe heard that one of those selected was married and had a family, he acted with holy boldness and spontaneity. The Franciscan priest took the man's place in the lineup and was sent to the starvation bunker. Two weeks later he was executed by means of lethal injection of acid.[17]

That took spizzerinctum.

Sprezzatura: Simultaneous Opposites

If spizzerinctum is important for initiating and sustaining high levels of participation, sprezzatura is key for creative and innovative participation—a participation that can become inspiration.

When people think of sprezzatura (the few that think of it at all), what comes to mind is something along the lines of the following exchange between Methodism's founder John Wesley and Beau Nash in Bath in 1739. Nash was not one of Wesley's fans. When he approached Wesley walking on a narrow pavement, Nash is said to have proclaimed, "I never make way for a fool."

Stepping aside, Wesley replied: "Don't you? I always do."

That's sprezzatura. But only a small part of it.

Sprezzatura is an inherently contradictory, even ironic, word: it means the ability to make hard things look easy, the effort to appear effortless, the grace of gawkiness, a tour de force performance designed not to look performative. Sprezzatura became the buzz word of high Renaissance culture, when people tired of affectations and staged behavior but still wanted life to be lived with nobility and grace.

In the Christian Eucharist, what is recalled is, precisely, a resounding worldly failure: the gruesome death, outside the city, of a man who ruled no kingdom, made no fortune, won no wars, and who failed to persuade the majority of his contemporaries that he had anything of value to say.

—Historian and Catholic Layman Eamon Duffy[18]

Authentic participation requires a diversity of participants: a swap meet of ideas, with people contributing their unique gifts, thoughts, and feelings, lighting the fuse of many an odd train of thought. The more diverse the participants, the more real and original the experience. Sprezzatura also involves the freedom to fail, a theology of risk that is seldom found in establishment religion's risk-free mentality. In fact, it could be argued that the church's greatest failing is its failure to fail.[19]

The key to sprezzatura is paradox, the audacious algebra of the spiritual, the natural language of faith. If one reason why the church isn't the most creative place around, it's the fear of living with contradictions, the inability to get it right in both directions. Sprezzatura is the magic word that opens heaven's doors and lets out Truth.

GROUNDS FOR TRUTH

Perhaps Jesus' habit of welcoming whatever person or circumstance life brought him, embracing spontaneity, helps explain why he was the most creative person ever to walk the earth. Creativity needs ambiguity, fuzziness, fluidity, diversity. What kills creativity? Certainty, clarity, homogeneity, and fixed boundaries. What fuels your creativity?

Sprezzatura brings together opposites. Authentic experiences of God must have the element of sprezzatura in them because biblical truth is itself paradoxical. The eternal, transcendent, omniscient God is made available to mere mortals. How can that be? Jesus, very God of very God, becomes sin for us. You must be kidding! The holy God sacrifices God's own flesh—God's Son—for the good of God's sworn enemies. You can't be serious!

For Christians, paradox is the midwife of truth.[20] Where did we ever get this notion that truth is clear and singular? Truth is better described as misty and multiple: it comes to those who are good at both standing still and journeying on.

Every time Jesus was finished talking, the disciples turned to one another and whispered, "Did you get that? Does anyone have any idea what he is talking about?" Or they turned to Jesus and said, "Master, what did you just say?" Jesus' goal was not that everyone understand him, but that everyone experience him. In fact, Jesus didn't expect everyone to get his revolutionary message.[21] He did invite everyone, however, to hear God's story, to become part of God's story, and to learn about others who joined God's story or were seeking God's presence. If you can put totally into words what you really mean, it's not Jesus talking. Jesus creates space in which we can enter into divine mystery and dangerous grace.

> *Paradox, scandal, and aporia are themselves nothing other than sacrifice, the revelation of conceptual thinking at its limit, at its death and finitude.*
>
> —FRENCH PHILOSOPHER JACQUES DERRIDA[22]

In fact, the essence of orthodoxy is what I call paradoxy. Biblical truth marries orthodoxy and orthopraxy into a union that Dwight Friesen calls orthoparadoxy.[23] In fact, the word *heresy* derives from the Greek word *choice:* choosing one truth to the exclusion of other truths. Heresy is the cross uncrossed: when the vertical and the horizontal no longer connect. Truth is when a body holds together its various parts in conversation and harmony. Truth is when opposites become not a battleground but a playground. That's why people of faith have such sharp noses for incongruities, ironies, and oxymoron.

BREWED FOR THOUGHT

"Our 'God is a consuming fire,' " reads Hebrews 12:29. But our experience of fire can either be the warmth of hearth and home, or a raging inferno of destruction and death. The "consuming fire" of God can either be our heaven or our hell.[24] When did God last consume you in comfort and warmth? When did God last consume you in destruction?

The resurrected Christ is both dead and alive. By taking scar tissue with him into eternity, Jesus announced that he is our dead and resurrected Lord. We like to talk about Jesus as our risen and regnant Lord, but that doesn't get it quite right. Better to speak of our crucified and risen Lord. But best of all, Jesus is our dead and resurrected Lord, our crucified and crowned Lord.[25]

We can't survive without sprezzatura. We live in three worlds simultaneously: our bodies, our spirits, and our souls. We can't choose to live in just one of these, or even two. We can only choose at what level to live in our bodies, our spirits, *and* our souls. But it's more complicated than that, since our material beings (bodies) have senses that perceive and conceive, and our nonmaterial beings (spirits) have minds that think and emotions that feel. And on top of those multiple existences that run in analog is the existence of our souls, which mix and digitize with the existence of our bodies and spirits in a four-dimensional world in all sorts of mysterious ways.

Søren Kierkegaard calls spiritual paradox the "passion of the infinite." Passion comes from the tug and tension of truth, the two infinite opposites pulling at one another: the objective and the subjective, intellect and emotion, solitude and communion, the past and the future, intimacy and distance, the on-the-way but not-there-yet journey of faith.[28]

> *Just as I can put my physical body into a garden of wonderful scents or into a stinking sewer, the same is true in the spiritual world. We each choose whether our lives will be a detective novel, a scandal sheet, or a scripture.*
>
> —RABBI ADIN STEINSALTZ[26]

> *The question is not whether we will be extremists, but what kind of extremists we will be. Will we be extremists for hate or will we be extremists for love?*
>
> —MARTIN LUTHER KING JR.[27]

TWO SIDES TO EVERY STORY

Richard Wagner was a great composer, and he was a disgusting human being. There is no split- or slit-the-difference approach to Wagner's life that will reconcile these two realities. D. H. Lawrence was a marvelous writer, and an appalling bigot. There is no one-way about it. He was both.

Saint Augustine described God as *semper agens, semper quietus:* "always active, always at rest." For Jesus, who embodied the apparently conflicting justice and mercy of his Father, God was first "Our Father," a relationship of intimacy. But no sooner had those words "Our Father" left his mouth than came the whiplash of distance: "who art in heaven." God is immanent (Emmanuel) and transcendent (Elohim). In Jesus Christ two things are revealed: God's incredible love for us and God's inscrutable will for us. Truth has two sides.

Every Christian is *simul justus et peccator:* "simultaneously saint and sinner." There is no middle path between the two. The Feast of All Saints on November 1 is immediately followed by the Feast of All Souls. All Saints' feast is for the saints. All Souls' feast is for *all* people who have died, whether Christians or not. Our bodies are going two opposite directions at the same time: catabolism works to tear it down, metabolism works to build it up. In your life and mine the forces of love and life work alongside opposing forces of hatred and death.

> *The wall of Paradise is built of contraries, nor is there any way to enter but for one who has overcome the highest spirit of reason who guards the gate.*
>
> —NICHOLAS OF CUSA,
> *De Visione Dei,* chapter 9[30]

In one of Jesus' many two-handers, he could say, "Let the dead bury the dead" on the one hand while on the other he could say, "Always go the extra mile."[29] Or look at the two answers he gave as to how to obtain eternal life: (a) to Nicodemus he said, "You must be born again," and (b) to the rich young ruler he said, "Sell what you have."

Jesus came at his ambidextrousness naturally: he was born a blue blood in the royal city of Bethlehem, and he grew up in the can-anything-good-come-out-of, blue-collar town of Nazareth. By lively shifting weight from one foot to the other, Jesus always landed with both feet on the ground.

Life is not truth or consequences. Life is truth *and* consequences. Truth will impact your life whether you accept it or deny it, whether you live it up or live it down. As my Gramma Boggs used to say, "Whether you get truth right or wrong, there will be consequences."

Passionate Coolness

Jesus didn't call the disciples to regular discipleship. Regular disciples would have stayed in Jerusalem, founded a school, studied the words and works of their master, carefully screened and admitted only the most promising students. But Jesus wasn't regular. He commanded his disciples to scatter, to go to the ends of the earth, preaching and teaching the good news, healing the sick, casting out demons, witnessing about the life, death, and resurrection of Jesus Christ.

Jesus' command ensured that the disciples would go out to the people, not sit and wait for an interested few to come to them. Jesus' command called his disci-

> *Under every no lay a passion for yes that had never been broken.*
> —USAMERICAN POET
> WALLACE STEVENS[31]

ples to be witnesses, not students, not caretakers, not sages. The disciples saw with their own eyes the miracle of the resurrection, the glory of the ascension, and they knew the significance of those acts. Their witness was to nothing less than the salvation of the world.

The calling that shaped the lives and work of the disciples reflects direct experience more than distanced intellect, action more than erudition, boldness and chutzpah more than careful planning and deliberation. The first-century disciples are a much closer fit to today's well-curve world than are the church's modern-era ways of thinking and doing.

Jesus made the extreme sacrifice on Good Friday. And he went to the edge of the ledge on Holy Saturday, into death and darkness itself. On Easter Sunday he blew the world wide open, exploding into birth a new creation, commissioning his disciples to follow him out to the edges of creation.

How willing are we to dip into the well

- at the edge of knowledge where scientists and ethicists ponder the implications of gene manipulation, stem cell research, and the many other life-sustaining/life-ending decisions?
- at the edge of violence where armies and terrorist factions battle over who will be most feared?
- at the edge of technology where computers begin to think and react like humans, where the line between biological and mechanical life seems to blur?
- at the edge of wilderness where the threat of extinction hovers over species, and the extermination of habitat endangers the ecosphere, making even our weather patterns more extreme?
- at the edge of mission where Jesus' name has never been heard, where his name is used only as a curse, in the most distant corners of the earth, in the hollowed-out hearts of our cities?
- at the edge of hope where people are dangling at the ends of their ropes, their heads in nooses of hopelessness and despair?

Jesus instructed his disciples to dip into the well to experience the gospel's unconditional life, unmerited grace, and unlimited hope. Will you draw water from the well, so that people can drink of the water of life?

Seven

Brands as Image Statements

ep_Ic: ★bux Is _Image-Rich

> In the beginning is the image: first imagination
> then perception; first fantasy then reality.
> —PSYCHOLOGIST JAMES HILLMAN[1]

Have you ever wondered why, when you dream, it's not a scene of you sitting in a chair reading a script, turning page after page of text that translates your dream into words? Have you ever had a dream in which you sat for an extended period of time and read something? I haven't.

Dreams aren't like that. They are far closer to going to a movie, and as soon as you enter the theater, you are on screen, playing a role in the scene. But it's not a projection of light on a flat screen. It's 3-D, with plot and action unfolding as you are carried along by the story.

A dream is not text, not verbal inscriptions on paper. It's CinemaScope, Technicolor, in surround sound with Dolby. We dream in images—sights, sounds, smells, motion. But why images and not words? In fact, research shows that while we're asleep, the portion of our brains that comprehends written language is dormant. We are effectively *unable* to read in our dreams. Perhaps that should tell us something about the nature of dreamers and how one might grab hold of a dreaming world's attention.

Da Vinci Was Right About Television

Chances are you were born in the Television Generation. And if you're younger than that, you were born to parents who were part of the TV Generation. Prior to the early 1950s, people got their news and entertainment primarily from reading or from the radio (after the mid-1920s). Movie theaters showed newsreels—short films carrying news of the day. But for most USAmericans, the standard mode of information was words. Words were the common currency of communication—either words printed on paper or words carried on radio waves. The words left the reader or listener to form his or her own pictures—mental pictures elicited by what was read or heard. It wasn't a bad system.

But then came television, and to say merely that television triggered a revolution is to say the sun is a little bit warm. This was a revolution of a magnitude that no one could have imagined. Television added both sound and pictures to words, and the combination was irresistible. Leonardo da Vinci predicted the tellyverse when he said that image and sound were the two perfect media, one conveying signals from the visible world, the other the invisible world, and that when the world truly brought them together nothing would be the same again.[2]

I have a friend who grew up in a small town in the Midwest. He was talking to an older man, a member of the Korean War generation, who was describing one of the first television sets to arrive in that town in the early 1950s. A shopkeeper set up the television in the display window of a Western Auto store, and it was such a novelty that townspeople would gather in front of the store after work just to watch the pictures on the television set.

BREWED FOR THOUGHT

Try this experiment: leave your television set turned off every morning for a week, and on those days pay close attention to how distracted you are while getting ready for work or school. Notice whether it's easier to get out the door on time and whether you spend less time hunting for things before you leave your home. The following week, leave the television turned on every morning. Once again, note your level of distraction, the number of things you can't locate (car keys, shoes, your wallet). And notice as well if you are leaving your home at a later time on the mornings when the television is left on. It's hard to walk past a television set that is on without stopping to watch. You are drawn to it, even if it's a commercial for paper towels. Television is a prime demonstration of the power of an image-rich medium to capture and hold your attention.

If someone had been at that same store reading a newspaper, a small crowd would never congregate to listen to him read. But introduce a television set and you'd better make room for some lawn chairs. And it wasn't just the novelty of the new technology that drew a crowd. Long after televisions became commonplace in USAmerica, the attraction was still undeniable. Children were mesmerized, and so were adults. Studies have been conducted to try to measure the impact of television on our culture. Findings from various studies have blamed television for everything from childhood obesity to attention deficit disorder to the decline in neighbors getting to know one another to sleep deprivation.

Can such a simple thing as television truly have brought about such a cataclysmic shift in society? Yes, it did. But how, and why? Primarily for one reason: television yokes images to words and sound. It's the images that make the difference. J. K. Rowling (pronounced "Rolling") is one of the most successful writers in all of history. But why? When kids are asked why her Harry Potter books appeal to them, the same response is heard over and over again: she writes in such a way that kids feel they are "watching them like a movie instead of reading them."[3]

GRANDE PASSION IN IMAGE-RICH METAPHORS

We live in an image-hungry, image-driven world. Life itself has become a motion picture. We are now living movies. We just aren't living the right ones. We settle for a bit part in a B movie, going through the motions of a story line that is rote and uninspiring. We sacrifice grande passion for the security of rules and the sameness of routine. When we could be the stars of a lifelong movie about EPIC passion, we trust facts and not parables, ideology and not imagery.

> *Man is primarily an image-maker and our psychic substance consists of images; our being is imaginal being, an existence in imagination. We are, indeed, "such stuff as dreams are made of."*
>
> —PSYCHOLOGIST JAMES HILLMAN[4]

But kids get it, even if adults don't. Stories constitute some of the richest images because stories paint pictures that come alive in your imagination. Award-winning children's author Philip Pullman, a zealous unbeliever, at least gets it right when it comes to the irresistible appeal of stories well told.[5] Pullman taught me that the future belongs to the storytellers, especially those who can build stories around arresting metaphors and compelling images.

In 1996 Pullman received England's highest honor for children's literature, the Carnegie Medal, for his *The Golden Compass*.[6] In his acceptance speech he argued that "there's more wisdom in a story than in volumes of philosophy." He continued,

> What characterizes the best of children's authors is that they're not
> embarrassed to tell stories. They know how important stories are.…
> Now I don't mean children are supernatural wise little angels gifted
> with the power of seeing the truth that the dull eyes of adults miss.
> They're not. They're ignorant little savages, most of them. But they
> know what they need, and they go for it with the intensity of passion,
> and what they need is stories. Why do they spend so much time
> watching TV? They're not watching documentaries about Eastern
> Europe or programs about politics. They're watching drama, film,
> story. They can't get enough of it.[7]

Words have power. Images have even more power. An EPIC experience generates power and attains an irresistible level of attraction through the richness of images. The essence of anything EPIC is the Big Picture. It's IMAX, not iPod. Starbucks uses minimal language, maximal picture. That helps explain the long lines.

ICONS OF IDENTITY

It's interesting to consider how we develop attachments to certain objects such as coffee mugs. The morning is not right unless we're drinking out of the right cup. When I'm home, coffee doesn't taste right unless it's in my eagle mug. When I'm on the road, coffee isn't just right unless it's in a paper cup with a bra.

Starbucks is a symbol as well as a reality, and it's as a symbol that its real power lies.

Think about the images of Starbucks: signage and image are central to what is known as the Starbuckization of culture. The first thing you see in that Starbucks cup you're holding is a green logo of what looks to be a mermaid or siren emerging from the water surrounded by a double circle. In early Christian sacred art, the sea (*Thalassa* in the Greek world, *Mare* in the Latin) was portrayed as a queenly female figure. In a remarkable coincidence, a Christian mosaic in the Church of the Apostles at Madaba in Jordan (AD 578) shows Thalassa rising from the water holding in her left hand a rudder, but her right hand forms a blessing. And around her is a double circle.[8] If you didn't know better, you would think this was the prototype of the Starbucks logo.

The Starbucks version of Thalassa, first chosen by the original Starbucks owners—Gordon Bowker, Jerry Baldwin, and Zev Siegel—invites the holder

BEAN THERE

Especially in premodern cultures, images were widely used to convey messages and brand identities. In 1506 Henry VII reduced the number of centuries-old stew houses (brothels) in the borough of Southwark, County of Surrey, from eighteen to twelve. But the ones he kept open had something going for them: well-established brand names such as Boar's Head, the Cardinal's Hat, the Cross Keys, the Gun, the Crane, the Swan, and the Bell.[9] It's not that far a stretch to today's shoppers reaching for Tony the Tiger or the Jolly Green Giant.

into a liquid universe of fluidity and fantasy. She has now joined a pantheon of iconic images, which in some ways carry a greater aura of significance than the products they promote:

- three-pointed star of Mercedes-Benz
- silver lady of Rolls-Royce
- black prancing horse of Ferrari
- propeller against a blue sky of BMW
- yin and yang of Pepsi
- swoosh of Nike

The mermaid's ancestors are the logo girls of my youth: the Morton Salt Girl, the White Rock Soda Maiden, the Coppertone girl, the Clabber Girl on the baking powder can, and the ethnic logo girls that I found more interesting as a young boy because they had breasts. That stellar lineup includes the Argo Corn Starch corn maiden, the Sun-Maid girl (the one on cigar boxes was the best), Contadina (the tomato paste girl), and Aunt Jemima.[10]

One of the most interesting brand images in history was the plaquette, an insert used by wealthier Christians to sip from drinking cups. These small plates, some plain, some made of silver gilt, had biblical scenes hammered into them so that whoever put the cup to his lips could not escape drinking in the gospel. To take a drink was to take in at the same time the greatest story ever told. In the Greek and Russian Orthodox traditions, communion cups to this day come with small enamel plaquettes on the sides conveying key images of the life of Jesus.

Has It Been "Starbucked"?

Brands are tattoos on the soul. Perhaps only Google and Rick Warren, who almost has a copyright on the word *purpose* (have you tried saying that word without thinking of Warren?), surpass Starbucks in brandland. The making of the Starbucks noun into a verb (for example, "Nobody has Starbucked the day spa experience"[11]) attests to its status as a power brand and to the company's branding genius. Starbucks's motto, "The best way to build a brand is one person at a time," has never been stated better.[12] In fact, it could be argued that the very success of Starbucks from day one is due mainly to its decisions to make baristas eligible for health and 401(k) benefits, and to spend more money on training staff than on advertising its product, giving it an employee-turnover rate so low it's legendary.[13]

Every Starbucks store is different, but the Starbucks image is the same wherever you go (with the exception of the original store in Seattle). Branding is now about image creation, and at almost every point of contact Starbucks brands on your brain an image that reflects its mission and uniqueness. Even when its plaquettes are print, you drink in the text, choosing to trust Starbucks amidst all the culture wars and media clutter.

Medieval culture understood the power of an image statement in the tradition of the coat of arms. When Pope Benedict XVI chose a seashell for his Episcopal coat of arms in Munich, Catholics understood the implicit reference to Augustine walking the seashore, picking up a seashell, and observing that our brains can no more contain the full knowledge of God than a seashell can contain the sea.

Starbucks has made its image statement, not as a power statement or a product statement, but as a spiritual statement. Starbucks stores fill empty space, and Starbucks cups fill white space, with spiritual significance. There are different words on the back of a Starbucks cup...many of them from religious and spiritual sources. (Starbucks recognizes that you cannot get wisdom about life without religious resources.) There are even life-enhancing quotes from celebrities as diverse as NBA guard Ray Allen and pastor Rick Warren. But the image statement (which may be a better way of talking about brands) stays on message, which has less to do with specific products and more to do with passion, loyalty, trustworthiness, customer service and satisfaction, and spiritual enrichment. A corporate mission can change over time (just ask IBM or AT&T) if its image statement remains strong and consistent.

In fact, the entire design environment of a Starbucks is an image statement of the Starbucks experience. There is lots of variety within that image statement, since every Starbucks is different. And the variety offers a sense of adventure every time you walk into a new one, and some surprise every time you visit a familiar one. Every Starbucks cheers up the soul by customizing itself for major holidays, religiously saving my favorite Christmas Blend for post-Thanksgiving release much like some Episcopalians save Christmas carols for post-Christmas singing.

But no matter how much variety is involved, you know from the informal atmosphere, festive decorations, aromatic surroundings, artsy lights, and comfy furniture that it's a Starbucks—your own personal VIP lounge. Even if they didn't put their name on the place, you'd know a Starbucks by the feel of its design environment. It's as distinctive (and addictive?) as the boudoir ambience of a Victoria's Secret shop or the humor of Southwest Airlines.

Unlike fast-food restaurants, Starbucks doesn't scream at you "I'm here." And in the quiet of a nonshouting brand, you recognize Starbucks's presence naturally and effortlessly. It works hard to fit into the neighborhood and suggests permanent, long-term residency rather than short-term, hit-and-run transience. Newer Starbucks stores mix open space and high ceilings with nook-like corners and crannies, catering to whatever mood you're in. One of my favorite strange-city "sports" is to drive neighborhoods and predict where the local Starbucks might be.

ETHICS AND IMAGE STATEMENTS

If the experience is the essence of the brand, the design is what helps create the experience. One big reason why Starbucks beats its competitors is that it is winning the war of the icons. In a world dominated by images, image warfare is the conflict of the future. And the victory goes to those who can make their experiences as accessible as possible through familiar and coherent images. A bad image can kill a product, a person, or a book. In fact, Barnes & Noble reserves the right to not stock a book in USAmerica if they dislike its cover.

Where Starbucks still needs to work on its image statement is in the ethical dimension of its brand, an area increasingly known as CSR (Corporate Social Responsibility), which encompasses both social betterment and environmental consciousness. The number of people throughout the world who depend on coffee for their livelihood has been estimated to be between twenty and twenty-five million.[14] How these laborers and family farms are treated is a social justice concern of the utmost importance; and, of course, it's part of Starbucks's bigger image statement. Starbucks stakeholders should be just as interested in progress toward fair trade as they are in free trade[15] if the mantra of "fair market coffee" is to be more than an invoking of some moral high ground in defense of one's dependency.

Starbucks boasts it is North America's largest purchaser of Fair Trade Certified coffee. Of all the retailers in North America, Starbucks sells more fair-trade coffee (marketed by co-ops that guarantee living wages to coffee growers) than anyone. It also says you can walk into any store and ask for a brewed cup of fair-trade coffee, and if the featured coffee of the day is not fair trade, they will brew a fair-trade blend for you. But while Starbucks will spend extra money buying fair-trade coffee,[16] they won't spend one extra dollar, pound, or euro educating customers about why on earth we should buy it. And while Starbucks will partner with Earvin "Magic" Johnson to put down stakes in eighty-seven urban locations, the Starbucks small-town cachet is more suburban than urban friendly.

Starbucks's green logo is their way of saying "green is green." But "green" means more than Paul Newman's marinara sauce or Ben & Jerry's Buzzachillo.

Companies in the future will be required to submit annual reports detailing ways in which they have been good corporate citizens. Many companies like Starbucks are now doing this voluntarily. In 2005, one-third of USAmerica's top one hundred companies issued voluntary SEE (social, environmental, ethical) standards and accountability reports on their social responsibility. But only one out of one thousand invited an outside auditor to verify the company's reports. In Great Britain, 70 percent of top companies issue social progress reports, half of which are verified by an independent monitor such as SAI (Social Accountability International), an accrediting agency that certifies the monitors of outsourced makers of toys, apparel, and other products.

It is at this juncture that image statement and text statement need to assist one another. While images shout loudly, and more and more it is images that take center stage in presenting compelling messages, sometimes an image statement needs to team up with straight text. Starbucks is in a unique position to educate the public; and fair-trade, environment-friendly coffee deserves our attention. A full and compelling explanation of these issues will need to go beyond image statement. It is here that images and words come full circle. Starbucks can supply the words that will open our eyes to the plight of coffee growers and coffee workers, and the related issues of poverty and creation care as they apply to coffee.

It's not either/or, image *or* words. It's both/and, image *and* words. The Word became flesh and dwelt among us. Jesus was a man (image) living among us. He was also text (the Word become flesh). And that leads us to reading the gospel in a Starbucks cup.

Eight

The Gospel in an Image-Rich Cup

God Speaks in More Than Just Words

The Word became flesh and made his dwelling among us.
—JOHN 1:14

God told the Hebrews they were a peculiar people. That doesn't mean they were odd, necessarily, but as God's chosen they were different, set apart. They were people of the covenant, and as such they were uncommon, distinct from every other nation. Monotheism is known nowhere else in antiquity and is a peculiar notion (hence a "peculiar" people).[1]

As we know from reading Scripture and history, this has been Israel's greatest blessing and its most dogged curse. Israel remains God's peculiar people whether they are in the wilderness, the promised land, carried off into exile, or back at home after nineteen hundred years away.

If you are a follower of God, you're peculiar as well. "Odd man out," we used to say. God-followers are not like other people. They have a different resonance to their lives, a different rhythm. They have a different understanding of both where they fit in the world and how they don't fit in the world.

Peculiarity, it could be argued, is ordained by God. We are a new-creation people, a people whose permanent home is a "new heaven and a new earth."[2] But talk to a nonChristian and you'll understand that "peculiar" is not all that far from "odd," and odd can come dangerously close to "strange" and even "scary." Oddness is an image that Christians regularly project, and it fails to make the message of Christianity more accessible. An image, after all, can be Jason from *Friday the 13th* just as easily as it can be Betty Crocker baking a batch of cookies. Misplaced Christian zeal has done an awful lot of damage throughout world history.

BREWED FOR THOUGHT

Think about the biblical images that make God immediate in your life, that bring God close. What are those images, and why do they enliven your spirit? Now, think about the biblical images that stir your passion for life. Do any of the same images appear on both lists?

In the gospel according to Starbucks, icons and images make the experience as accessible as possible. They invite you in, urging you to join yourself to the experience that is framed by the images. You won't find images of exclusion. Instead, the imagery is familiar and coherent. You can't mistake a Starbucks, whether it's a standalone store, a corner of a supermarket, a kiosk in an airport, or a future-fitting of an old bank in Columbus, Ohio.

Faith is the same way. You can't avoid having images frame your spiritual life. At the heart of Christianity is the use of images as well as words. The question is this: how can Christians make the imagery of faith so identifiable, so accessible, so unmistakable, that faith can't be confused with anything else? It's not ritual, dogma, religion, or

> *Don't roast your coffee beans*
> *in the marketplace.*
> *[Don't cast pearls before swine.]*
> —OROMO NOMAD PROVERB

spiritual weirdness. It's authentic experience made personal through our full participation in what God is doing. And all of this is empowered by vivid imagery.

Aleksandr Solzhenitsyn concluded his 1970 Nobel lecture on literature by quoting a Russian proverb: "One word of truth outweighs the whole world."[3] In our culture, it's more true that one image of truth, and especially one Person of truth, tilts the balance of history. People today are like the Israelites in the desert: they'll follow a cloud or a pillar of fire, but not abstract commands and disembodied voices. We want music, not math; poetry, not polemics. Once, God became fire and cloud. Then God became flesh. God did not become a PowerPoint presentation in the sky.

"Sinners in the Hands of an Angry God" is perhaps the most famous sermon in USAmerican history. If people outside the church know about one sermon, it's this one. Why do we remember it? It's not the content or the theology. It's Jonathan Edwards's unforgettable imagery of people as spiders dangling by a thread over the flames of hell. Once you see that image in your mind it's hard to discard it. Or think about a searing image from this century. One television image, the Twin Towers falling into dust and rubble, can make an isolated terrorist group hiding out in mountain caves look pretty impressive. Try to dismiss the mental picture of a commercial jetliner crashing into the second tower. You can't.

THE MASTER OF METAPHOR

Lest you fear that I'm minimizing the centrality of God's self-revelation through the words of Scripture, let me put the idea of rich imagery in context. A Christian's faith is not impassioned by the correctness of a carefully constructed dogma or the logic of an unassailable verbal argument. But faith is set on fire by the images that the words of Scripture present.

The power of the Word to move people from rote religion to full-life immersion is not in the words themselves. It's in the images, the stories, the music of Scripture. Before there was any matter, there was God. The universe existed as an image in God's passion before the universe existed as a creation.

Genesis tells us that God made "every plant of the field before it was in the earth, and every herb of the field before it grew."[4] Since the mind is made of metaphors (remember, we dream in pictures, not in text), the greatest power over others is the power held by those who choose the metaphors. Jesus was history's greatest master of metaphor. In his metaphors lie metamorphosis. The metaphors we live in become the reality we live out.[5]

BREWED FOR THOUGHT

Think about the metaphors that guide your life. Are they Jesus metaphors, such as the overjoyed father who runs to welcome a lost child back home? Or are they manmade metaphors that point you in a direction other than Godward?

What made Einstein such a genius? It wasn't just that he thought in images (we all do). It was that he was consciously thinking in images and using the images to move his thoughts. As a teenager, Einstein was hounded by this image: "What would we see if we could keep pace with a beam of light?" And from that image of riding a beam of light came the theory of relativity.

THE MIND OF GOD

Metaphor is more than a linguistic tool; it's a cognitive attribute. Pulpit-centric preachers learned how to exegete words. But EPIC preaching delivers the passion of images. By exegeting images, a preacher leads his or her listeners into mystery and becomes the steward of the one Metanarrative—Jesus.[6] Image-rich communicators are first and foremost midwives of metaphor.[7]

BREWED FOR THOUGHT

Picture yourself in a future time when every person on earth has a personal mantra—three words or less that captures the essence of his or her mission. What would your mantra be?

It's correct to consider the image-rich Scriptures as the mind of God made available to us. The Bible "thinks," not in propositions and bullet points, but in images, metaphors, narratives, symbols, and song. Poetry is more the language of biblical faith than prose or philosophy. The church's failure of imagination is directly attributable to its failure to take up the poet's tools: image and imagination, metaphor and story, and metaphor stories known as parables.

When you read the Bible, do you look for the thesis statement, the main principle, or the key idea? Or do you look for the image that will change your life, the leading or controlling metaphor that reframes the conversation or story? This metaphor can be a character, a key moment in the story, an artifact (prop) or artifice, even a word that functions as an image. Metaphor is not simply an adornment to critical insight, but a method of perception in itself. Metaphors are not life's seasoning; they're the very meat of life.

Just like every computer is simply hardware until it is formatted by software, metaphors format life. The question is whether we will choose metaphorical software that will format our lives on a soul-growing or soul-destroying grid. The controlling metaphors control life, either toward the passion of God or away from it.

We live in a visual culture that speaks in images more than words. Advertisers spend billions of dollars a year, not to bombard us with words, but to surround us with images. Christianity begins and ends in an image: Jesus is the image of God, the logo of the Logos. In the beginning was the Logos which became Logo. In the end we will be nothing but logos that become Logos, human images that become spittin' images of God. Image is potentially much more redemptive than word.

> As God hath spangled the firmament
> with starres, so hath he his Scriptures
> with names and Metaphors,
> and denotations of power.
> —John Donne[8]

FLESHING OUT THE POWER OF WORDS

In this emphasis on metaphor and imagery, there are two things that should not be forgotten. First, if you ever start thinking that words are unimportant and don't need to be carefully selected, consider this: there is a big difference between someone yelling "Fire!" and someone screaming "Conflagration!" Anyone got a conflagration extinguisher? And on another note, I'm not sure we would still be singing "Amazing Grace" if John Newton's original title had held sway: "Faith's Review and Expectation."

Second, don't forget that every community has sacred words, a sacred vocabulary that needs to be learned. Even Starbucks expects you to learn its language.

Jesus gets us to speak a new language, a language that has many accents, the language of faith. Yale historian of Christian doctrine Jaroslav Pelikan, who died in 2006, was asked by Harvard University Press to write something autobiographical. So he produced a book that was actually a glossary of the theological words and phrases that shaped his soul. His autobiography was the language of faith that made him who he was. He called it *The Melody of Theology.*

Contrary to the emphasis of some of the more contemporary Bible translations, it was not Peter's Galilean accent that singled him out as a confederate of Jesus. "Surely you too are one of them; for even the way you talk gives you away."[9] Yes, Peter spoke with the characteristic drawl of a Galilean, but that is not why he was associated with Jesus. His speech, meaning the diction of his spiritual passion, is what linked him with the Word made flesh. Is our speech

> *Surely thou also art one of them;*
> *for thy speech betrayeth thee.*
> —MATTHEW 26:73, KJV

betraying us that we too are followers of Jesus? Does our language lump us in with some other camp, rather than with the Savior? At the very least, Scripture ought to be the language in which Christians talk to one another.

THE THINGY-FICATION OF WORSHIP

Metaphor is by definition experiential, interactive, and relational. EPIC worship is at its best when it turns images into what I call thingys,[10] and when those thingys become interactive icons that people can take home. With such a tangible and tactile icon, worshipers can later pick up and caress the texture of what they have committed to.

Jesus was a master at using props. In the story of the trap set for him by the Pharisees, the questions relate to paying tribute to Caesar. Jesus makes the Pharisees display a coin with Caesar's image stamped on it. By having them produce the coin, Jesus springs the trap on them. The Pharisees have proven they are willing to employ and deploy an idol, a graven image, which was specifically forbidden by Jewish law. Jesus' both/and answer ("Give to Caesar what is Caesar's, and to God what is God's") typifies metaphor's multivalence: Pharisees and Romans alike could feel that he was supporting them, while Jesus was telling them two things at once; one, that the Pharisees were asking the wrong question, and two, that they needed to be pointed in the right direction.

Starbucks is full of thingys—mugs, water bottles, plates—that are already becoming as collectible as Coca-Cola artifacts. While we must not worship any thing, the life of faith needs thingys to help it flex its muscles. The virtual nature of so much of our culture is making us even more hungry for tactile, iconic, multisensory experiences and thingys to hang on our walls and bodies. Faith is itself a brand, an identifier that sets us apart, singling us out as a peculiar group of people.

Doing Your Thing Must Not Become a Thingy

Shortly before her death, Mother Teresa of Calcutta was asked why she spent her life caring for the dying. "Because I like doing my own thing," she replied. In this one response, Mother Teresa had captured the meaning of Augustine's famous dictum, "Love God and do what you will." When we share God's heart of love, our wills will be God's will. Doing our own things will be doing the divine thing.[11]

There is natural resistance to the thingy-fication of faith, especially among Protestants. Didn't Jesus say you can't serve God and Mammon? Isn't there a danger that our thingys could get in the way of doing the divine thing?

You bet they can. John Calvin rightly warned that "the human mind is a perpetual forge of idols," which is why he banned any use of visual imagery in the conveyance of divine truth. Of course, Calvin failed to see that the printed word could become as much of an idol as any icon, and the whitewashing of churches—even those without a crucifix—is still a visual image. Two of the greatest iconoclastic acts of our time reveal the twenty-first-century fear of images as idols: the Taliban destruction of the Bamiyan Buddhas (destroyed as an emblem of Hazara identity) and Al Qaeda's destruction of the Twin Towers (destroyed as images of global capitalism). Both acts of destruction are expressions of the residual sensitivity of religious traditions to things as idols. We are living in a world of iconoclash, the war of the images, or in the case of fundamentalism, the war against images.

BREWED FOR THOUGHT

What are you doing to reveal the spiritual through the natural and the material of your life? Are you doing your own thing or the divine thing?

But here are two things to keep in mind about thingys. First, Jesus' word for "mammon" literally means "money." Not materiality, but "money."

Second, the incarnation is God's way of affirming our thinginess. We ourselves are things, or as Aquinas would have it, "gift-things." And the bodily resurrection of Jesus affirms the fact that some form of thinginess will accompany us into eternity. God places value on artifacts. Or, as Paul puts it, "The spiritual did not come first, but the natural, and after that the spiritual."[12] The spiritual comes in and through the natural; divinity, through humanity.

CELEBRITY CULTURE

If you still doubt the power of the image, then consider the rise of celebrity culture. Try to say the names Sinatra, Greta Garbo, Judy Garland, or Elvis without spraying some pixie dust.[13]

The tendency to worship artists and athletes is not a new phenomenon, to be sure. What can only be called a cult following formed around Franz Liszt, often cited as the greatest of all pianists. In this Liszt cult, wealthy, well-bred European women would collect clippings from his flowing white mane and even wear his discarded cigar butts on their clothes as fashion accessories. And when the jousting match replaced the melee as the chief warrior sport in the thirteenth century, a new type of celebrity arose that made it possible for people of humble origins to rise to wealth and fame.[14]

Few subjects I talk about with religious leaders generate more defensiveness than the pervasiveness of celebrity culture and the power of celebrities to exercise a mesmeric effect on the rest of us. Pastors from rural areas tell me how far removed this is from their contexts. That is, until I ask them to read their own small-town markers. When you enter Fairmount, Indiana, off Route 69, there is a huge sign proudly announcing that this little town is the "Home of James Dean and Garfield."

After I listen patiently to the obligatory denunciations of celebrity culture, I then gently change the subject to how the pitchers on their favorite baseball teams are doing. What follows is a torrent of sports stats and stories that betrays an acquaintance with athletics that straddles the border between fan and fanatic. When high-powered executive types denounce the Hollywood Star System, I then bring out a copy of *Fortune* magazine or *Business 2.0* and start reading the articles, which are as star-studded as any *Star* magazine. Or I get out my favorite business rag, *Fast Company*, and observe how the keys to rating books on a 0–5 scale can't be done any longer with gold stars or platinum images, but need celebrities to go along with them: "Clarity of Writing" is attached to Malcolm Gladwell ("Gladwellian prose"); "Soundness of Logic" is attached to James Surowiecki ("Surowieckian reason"); and "General Prescience" is attached to Thomas L. Friedman ("Friedmanian foresight").[15]

BREWED FOR THOUGHT

Think about some of the churches you have recently worshiped in. Has the rich, provocative image of Christianity been replaced by sterile, neutered spaces that seem more like physicians' waiting rooms than temples?

The two places in the church that denounce celebrity culture the most are seminaries and emerging church/Emergent circles. Yet the role of big personalities looms as large if not larger in emerging/Emergent churches as in more traditional ones. In spite of all the talk of teamwork, can you name me one Emergent "team"? Can you name one emerging church that is not pastored by a strong image or striking personality?[16] In spite of all the egalitarian, communal ideals, when the rubber hits the road, Acts 4:32 crashes head-on with the power of celebrity dynamism.

Mediated culture is taking the cult of celebrity in new directions. James Bond was the creation of Ian Fleming. But Fleming admitted that even he began to write his later novels with Sean Connery in mind. Ever meet a Moon Man? The twelve men who've set foot on the moon, known collectively as the Moon Men, have a common problem. They get large fees for appearing at Star Trek conventions. But the television actors from Star Trek tend to draw bigger crowds than the *real* Moon Men.

In celebrity culture, person becomes personality, and Jesus becomes a superhero. Check out the Christ allusions in the Superman, Spider-Man, or X-men movies, or the more veiled but equally forceful Jesus-as-superhero dimensions to *The Lord of the Rings, Pirates of the Caribbean,* or even *The Passion of the Christ.*[17]

> *And those celebrities, competing of the judge's attention and approval, are in effect inviting the treatment they get. They are so needy, actually—dressing up, dieting, touring, posing, exposing privacies, cavorting desperately, endlessly, before us. In a way, at a certain level, celebrities are pathetic, undignified, utterly dependent. No, don't underestimate the unconscious sense of sovereignty that is the lot of spectators.*
>
> —THOMAS DE ZENGOTITA[18]

Celebrity worship is a part of our culture—or should I say *cult*—and it's not going away any time soon. So should the church learn to play the celebrity card? This is an especially difficult question to answer because celebrity worship is already a full-fledged religion. And there are forms of that religion that can be dangerous: one new "disorder" discovered by the psychiatric community is being called CWS for Celebrity Worship Syndrome.[19]

GRANDE FAITH IN A CELEBRITY CULTURE

Here are three considerations in pursuit of an image-rich faith that is incarnate in a celebrity culture.

Faith That Is Global and Local

First, another kind of spirituality is being born that isn't congregation based, but is instead EPIC based. New kinds of community are being formed that are both global and local at the same time.[20] In fact, for something to be real or global, it must be local. The Incarnation shows how Jesus saved the world by taking the local seriously. He wept over locals: once over a local person (Lazarus) and once over a local place (Jerusalem).

Osama bin Laden understands this *glocal* world and is building Al Qaeda accordingly. Bin Laden knows how to use local images to convey his global message: why do you think he broadcasts his messages from caves and cavernous regions in Afghanistan? It's a clear reference to the cave in which the Prophet received his first revelation. Bin Laden knows he is a media celebrity[21] and has learned how to use the technology of fax machine, computer terminal, and satellite dish to become a brand name with franchises all over the world—each franchise as skilled at opening up new branches as Subway. Palestinian journalist Abdel Bari Atwan calls bin Laden's mastery of modern communications cyber-jihad.[22] The only person who drives book sales more than Osama is Oprah.

Pope John Paul II understood the power of image, and he facilitated the resurgence of new forms of papal Christianity. When he decided to address the blight of AIDS, he first commissioned the writing of a papal encyclical about the AIDS crisis. Then he thought better of the idea. "If it doesn't happen on TV, it doesn't happen," he observed. So instead he called Mother Teresa and invited her to Rome to open an AIDS center.[23] And the whole world showed up. Pope John Paul II could fill the basilica. The Pope could fill any coliseum or stadium in the world. But he couldn't fill the churches. The Catholic churches of Europe remain empty.

Tell opera it doesn't need celebrity singers. We now have prima donna everything—celebrity historians, CEOs, hair stylists, chefs, architects, nannies, trainers. There are even celebrity anglers, thanks to tens of thousands hooked on fantasy fishing leagues. The leading celebrity angler earned $547,000 in 2005. And don't think the Protestant church is without its celebrities. Try to tell the evangelical world it didn't need its superpope named Billy Graham and other "papal" celebrities, such as James Dobson and Pat Robertson, to keep it together the past fifty years.

Recognize Who's a Celebrity

Second, maybe instead of attacking and bemoaning the narcissism of celebrity culture we ought to help everyone become a celebrity. In our world, anyone can be a celebrity, and nobodies can become instant celebrities. In fact, this globalization of the tribal was predicted by the famed Columbia University anthropologist Robert Murphy, who summed up the difference between modern and premodern societies in this way: "Everyone is famous in a tribe."[24] In premodern society everyone was a celebrity, due to being known in the neighborhood and known for something, whereas in modern society only the elite qualified for celebrity status.

It's not as if we're not already celebrities to begin with. To be born a USAmerican is to begin life as a celebrity. We live like kings used to. We have won first prize in the lottery of life. The only question is how we invest our lottery winnings.

It's also not as if we're not already thinking of ourselves as celebrities. Have you checked out Facebook, MySpace, or any number of other social networking sites? Have any people under thirty not already posted their photos and preferences (music, photo, and video libraries), and presented themselves as celebrities? If you go online for only a few minutes you see that not only are people writing ads for products they like, they are becoming the ads themselves: image icons.

Perhaps Christians need to be known not for being anti-celebrity but for celebrating a certain kind of celebrity: less handsome or beautiful and more compassionate and loving. Maybe Christians are the ones who give the laurel crown to those who do the least harm and most good. Maybe instead of focusing on celebrity power to attract adherents, Christians should focus on celebrity power to give away. Whereas we now worship those most adept at speaking the language of mediated culture, our ancestors worshiped everyman, the ordinary Joe, the common man—all descriptions of masses of people where single individuals didn't rise too far above the crowd. Maybe a celebrity culture is God's way of curing us of our fear of heights, our ambition to have no ambition. After all, standing on heights is different from standing on a pedestal.

If we're all celebrities, then Christians need to be highly visible in the culture. We need to be known as icons of passionate faith. Christians are not celebrities for themselves, but celebrities for Jesus. It is important that Christians not shirk from serving as high-profile figures to incarnate the gospel in this image-rich world. But as icons of Christ we invite others to see through us to God, the gospel, beauty, truth, and goodness.

And if we're all celebrities, then before we see humans as sinners, perhaps we should see them as God made them: as icons of God, cracked icons to be sure, but icons waiting their animation in the light. It makes all the difference in the world whether humans are depicted as simply sinners or whether sin is the condition and behavior of a cracked icon. Instead of regarding those outside the faith as sin personified, what if we saw them as fellow bearers of God's image who are marred by sin, as we all are?

De-idolize the Idols

Third, we idolize what we admire. Writers idolize writers. Athletes idolize athletes. Maybe Christians need to help idols de-idolize their lives and become icons. This is the only way we can play the celebrity card without falling into the celebrity trap.

Icons are different from idols, fetishes, or totems. You pray to an idol, fetish, or totem.[25] You pray through an icon. An icon is a window through which you look to God, a "painted window onto paradise."[26] If celebrities were true flesh-and-blood icons, we would see right through them. They would become magnifying glasses through which we see God. But instead, celebrities are fetishes, or idols, or totems. They obscure what's beyond them so attention focuses on them. They absorb all the light that comes their way rather than deflect it away from themselves and reflect it back on us and forward on God.

Our hope is not in idols. Our hope is in God. The only demands idols make on us is greater devotion. But icons, by inviting us to look through them to God, make us more wise and good and holy, and more dependent on God. Idolatry happens when the distinction between image and reality is lost.

BREWED FOR THOUGHT

Who acts as an icon in your life, inviting you to look through him or her to God? As a result of this relationship, do you notice yourself becoming more dependent on God?

In Nietzsche's classic *The Twilight of the Idols,* he proposed a strategy of sounding out idols with the "tuning fork" of critical or philosophical language.[27] Hit them hard enough to make them resonate, Nietzsche advised, but don't hit them so hard you smash them.

Christians need an EPIC tuning fork to use in sounding out the idols. Instead of critical reason alone we must use Jesus Christ, God's Perfect Pitch, as the tuning fork to the eternal. Our form of divination is not a philosophy but a Person: by striking images, we can see which images resonate with truth and which don't. The tuning fork of Jesus the Christ breaks the idol's silence and makes it tell the truth so that it reveals its true nature.

THE FINAL LETTER OF EPIC

Passionate spirituality is fully EPIC: Experiential, Participatory, Image-rich, and finally, Connective. Drinking coffee in isolation might be great when it's your first cup of the day. But have a cup at Starbucks and you'll never be alone. Coffee and people—groups of people, large and small, loud and quiet, playing chess or talking, the two go together like steam and espresso.

Like meeting a friend for coffee, the EPIC life is connective. It connects you to God and to others. So let's turn the page and get connected.

Nine

Your Undeniable Thirst for Connection

epi<u>C</u>: Starbucks Is <u>C</u>onnective

> There is in this world no real delight
> (excepting those of sensuality) but exchange
> of ideas in conversation.
> —SAMUEL JOHNSON[1]

Time for a quick coffee quiz. What do you enjoy more, a quiet cup of coffee alone in the morning, while you read the paper before leaving for work, or meeting good friends over coffee to get caught up on everyone's life? I'm sure you enjoy both, but which experience rises to the top? For most of us, an experience is enhanced far beyond the ordinary simply by sharing it with someone else.

For most of us, it's best that we have our first cup in the morning alone, before we engage with others. Early in the day, especially, coffee has a civilizing effect. But being civilized involves joining civilization, and that is where coffee excels. Talking one on one with a friend over coffee, or meeting for coffee with a small group of colleagues or friends, is hard to beat. Coffee is a communal drink, the Baptist beer.

Coffee connects people, and it helps people connect. Far from the dulling effects of alcohol, the other traditional communal beverage, coffee sharpens our wits. Even decaf has a way of opening our eyes to the day, to what's going on around us. If coffee is a civilizing drink, it's also a clarifying drink. It's easier to think, to ponder, to consider and reconsider with a cup of coffee in hand. That's why coffee and rational discourse have always gone together: coffee sharpens wits, clears minds, and enhances the power of connections.

CONNECTING FOR A BETTER EXPERIENCE

As coffee connects us, it invites us to a better experience—a shared experience. Otherwise why would people meet for coffee? You wouldn't go out of your way to schedule an appointment for shared misery over a cup of coffee. But you do regularly put coffee dates on your PDA in anticipation of a good experience. And often, given the EPIC nature of the gospel according to Starbucks, it's a warm, connective experience.

Coffee brings people together. That's why we don't have an idiom in the

GROUNDS FOR TRUTH

Look at your calendar for the next month and note which appointments involve coffee. How many of these appointments are you looking forward to? How many will involve reconnecting with people you don't see often enough?

English language along the lines of, "Let's stay apart for coffee." It's always, "Let's get together for coffee." And isn't getting together what makes us human, the social bond that we share as fellow creations of God? And in fact, it goes far deeper than merely a social bond. It's a relational and spiritual bond, the meaningful connection that we all seek with others.

Connecting with those around us isn't mere social convention, and it's not obligatory face time. Connecting connotes the interpersonal dynamic of enjoying and appreciating one another. It can include the welcome chemistry of finding a new friend and reconnecting with an old friend.

CONNECTING IN THE EPIC LIFE

In the EPIC life, connecting puts an exclamation point on all that precedes it. The experience that kicks off the EPIC life is attention grabbing, and that experience becomes meaningful when we participate in it. As we participate, the experience grows in importance, and we recognize and read the images that add richness to the meaning. And all of this serves as a preamble of sorts to the fourth element of the EPIC life: connection.

> *The information economy is not about the information or the economy. Everything important that happens there is about the relationship.*
> —SCIENCE FICTION AUTHOR AND ESSAYIST BRUCE STERLING[2]

What is it people want most? What is it we all are searching for most desperately? The answer is one word with a million meanings: connectedness. If you question that all people are seeking connection, all you need to do is log on to the Internet, the most important medium in the world. Use of the World Wide Web exploded not because of fascination with bells-and-whistles technology or because of online pornography, but because people discovered a new way to connect with others. The Internet may be a virtual community, but still it's a community that's readily available in a disconnected world. It delivers connectedness right to your laptop.

BREWED FOR THOUGHT

How often do you seek community and connection on the Internet? Are you involved in file sharing, social networking, group-edited Web sites, and so forth? What does virtual community on the Internet add to your life?

You can easily document this search for togetherness in online file sharing, blogs,[3] group-edited sites called wikis, social networking services such as Meetup, MySpace, and eHarmony. Social networking costs nothing on the Internet, but people have proven they are willing to pay for togetherness. People will buy just about anything if it promises connection. They'll even buy isolation if it promises connection.

But in typical well-curve fashion, the more we have virtual connections, the more we long for face-to-face, and even in-your-face, connections. The postmodern world's capacity to multiply connections and magnify disconnectedness sweeps people into solitary journeys with many "contact us" invitations. But contacts are not relationships. Even those most iglooed in their Outlook must break out of their desktops. In the words of Paul Ginsborg, "In each of their lives, there comes a moment of verification, when 'non-places' are not enough.... For, sooner or later, individuals need to measure themselves against reality, to obtain external proof, to try and decide on forms of conduct."[4]

You can see this in the de-mallification of America. When is the last time you went to a traditional mall? Did you see how empty it is? By traditional I mean old style, first-tier malls (built in the early 1960s) that cater to individuals and retail commerce, not to experiences of connectedness.

All the new madeover malls are moving on EPIC fronts. They are mixed-use (business, residential, child-care, education, restaurants) experience centers that bring back small-town street life. Barnes & Noble and Gap are only two of many chains that now refuse to invest in malls that face inward rather than outward onto streets and public spaces where people can stroll in "Main Street" environments. Malls that do not transition from shopping centers to sites that foster connection and community have no future.

READING CONNECTION ON A STARBUCKS CUP

We began this book by reading not a written text, but a cup. In particular, a Starbucks cup. At this point you might wonder if we have lost our way, wandering far from the path of grande-passion faith.

You might be asking: where do you read about connecting with others on a Starbucks cup? Well, think of where you buy the cup. Starbucks gives away a free living room for you to use while enjoying your beverage. Thirty-three million people stop in weekly and hang out in those comfy chairs and couches. And for those who buy something while hanging out, the average tab is only four dollars. In other words, Starbucks gives away a third place for very little money. This low-cost (to you) space is not the office and it's not your home. It's a much-needed third place where you connect with others in a different way.

Howard Schultz was one of the first to comprehend the concept of the third place when ethnologist Ray Oldenburg first elaborated it. Three places define and shape who you are: home, work, and a third place for community experiences. For Oldenburg the essential requirements of a third place include the following:

- It is neutral ground.
- It is inclusive and promotes social equality.
- Conversation is the central activity.
- It is frequented by regulars who welcome newcomers.
- It is typically in a nonpretentious, homey place.
- It fosters a playful mood.[5]

Church used to be a third place of choice, a meeting house, a sacred space where the community gathered for governing, for mourning, for celebrating, for relationship building. But churches increasingly became not relational space but propositional place. Instead of going there to connect with God and with others in meaningful relationship, people started going to church to be convinced of transcendent truth, or, if they already numbered among the convinced, to have their beliefs and religious convictions confirmed from the pulpit.

> *Without [the third place], the urban area fails to nourish the kinds of relationships and the diversity of human contact that are the essence of the city.*
>
> —RAY OLDENBURG[6]

The church lost credibility as a place for sacred relationship when it chose to specialize in formulating and advancing a better spiritual argument. The result is that people who came to the meeting house got connected with ideas and formulas more than they did with God and with other people.

And make no mistake, in all realms of life people are seeking meaningful connection. Bono is the world's most famous rock star. He is the lead singer for U2, which some have argued is the greatest rock group of the twentieth century, greater even than the Beatles and the Rolling Stones.

U2 has abandoned the theatrics it introduced into rock performances in the 1980s and '90s. Gone are the forty-foot lemons covered in mirrors, the gigantic olives on a toothpick, the belly dancers, the constant costume changes, the calls to the White House. Instead of bloated stagecraft, there is now only a simple metal stage with a seventy-three-foot extension designed to follow the radial lines of the heart—a heart that pierces the general admittance section of the audience, enabling Bono to walk into the crowd and connect with fans sitting in the cheapest seats.

BREWED FOR THOUGHT

Where is your favorite third place? It doesn't have to be a coffee shop, of course. It can be any place that is not home and not the workplace. Is your church a meaningful third place? If so, what does it do to fill that need? If your church fails as a sacred space for connection, what is missing?

The focus is now on the relationship of the musicians with the people. Bono believes people come to concerts less for great musicianship than for the experience of a relationship with musicians. This makes a concert less a performance than a conversation and opportunity for connection. U2's concerts are designed to invite people to experience and participate in the power of connectedness that can transform the world. In fact, Bono's new humanitarian organization is called DATA, which stands for Debt, AIDS, Trade for Africa.[7]

WE THIRST FOR A THIRD PLACE

The missing third place was the missing ingredient in the Starbucks philosophy, and Schultz reinvented Starbucks to give the world what it had lost when it abandoned cafés, salons, city plazas, main streets, and front porches. Starbucks designed stores that studiously avoid fast-food signals and encourage lingering and lounging. Where else can you stay as long as you like?

Over a thirty-year period, brewing your own Starbucks rather than buying coffee by the cup, you can save about fifty-five thousand dollars (if you factor in interest). But the buying habits of Starbucks lovers prove that some things in life are more important than money. Starbucks realized that people are starved for good coffee and good conversation. In a culture without a front porch, in a culture where we built up the backs of our houses with decks and walls, not the fronts of our houses where we might connect with a passing neighbor; in a world where we invested in privacy over hospitality, Starbucks spoke these words: "We'll be your front porch. Hang out here."

But third places are more than communal lobby lounges or places where porch sitters can combine food, conversation, computers, chairs, and couches.

> *What I do like most about Starbucks is sitting in a comfortable chair with my latte by my laptop. It's a great work environment when trying to study. I almost like studying there better than I do at the library.*
>
> —FRESHMAN CHEMISTRY MAJOR
> OLIVIA DIPACE[8]

People also want "public privacy." Starbucks has places for people to hang out partly because people don't want to hole up in their rooms and/or office cubes. People want spaces that combine both private and public. That's why all over the world hotel lobbies are being reinvented to feel more like airport club lounges and Starbucks. Even front desks are being eliminated for self-check-in kiosks and podiums manned by staffers. Most tellingly, in the last fourteen years, the number of new single-family homes that are built with front porches has increased from 42 to 53 percent.[9]

Remember the essence of a karaoke culture? The opportunity is there for anyone who wants to participate. If you want to take the stage and sing, grab the microphone. But most people don't choose to turn into momentary entertainers. They like the option of becoming Beyoncé or Bruce Springsteen for the duration of a pop song, but for most people just knowing it's an option is enough.

The same is true of Starbucks customers. It turns out that only 30 percent of customers actually use the tables and couches. But the notion that they could if they would keeps bringing them back. I have never once sat down to read a newspaper or just hung out at Starbucks. (I have scheduled appointments there, however.) But I have never once placed an order without looking around at all those chairs and finding comfort in the thought, "I could if I would. They're here if I need them." I only have this feeling with one other place: monasteries.

Virtual Connection with a Voice

Before we leave our more-exegetical probe of a Starbucks cup, one more observation. If Starbucks is held in one hand, many times the other hand is holding a cell phone. Like the popularity of coffee shops and virtual community on the Internet, cell phones embody another symptom of the human hunger for connection. They are everywhere. The first buyers of cell phones were wealthy and white. Less than twenty years later, more than half of all USAmericans, 150 million people, have mobile phones. And the number is growing at 15 percent a year.[10] Today's typical user? Women and African

Bean There

Don't you love watching movies from the 1980s (or earlier)? Where did all those pay phones come from? In those movies, it's not unusual even for police officers and undercover agents, hot on the trail of a criminal or spy, to rely on pocket change and a corner pay phone to call headquarters. When was the last time you used a pay phone? Have you *ever* used a pay phone?

Americans and teens. By the year 2001, 65 percent of African Americans had cell phones (62 percent of whites), and by early 2002, half of all teenagers between twelve and seventeen had cell phones. (It's now a rite of passage at age sixteen, or earlier, like getting a driver's license.) Parents like kids to have cell phones because it safely permits them to get farther away from home; kids love cell phones because it helps them get closer to friends.

If cell phones are everywhere in the developed world, they are exploding in the developing world. China is the world's largest market for mobile phones; Africa is the fastest growing. Bangladesh's famous "telephone ladies" rent out mobiles by the minute, putting phones into the hands of the poorest. The oft-quoted statistic that two-thirds of the world's population has never made a phone call is now an urban legend.[11] You now find cell phones where modern landlines were never installed: in the favelas of Brazil, the squatter camps of South Africa, the remote game farms of Africa. You even find bone-shaped cell phones around the necks of dogs. People want to be connected—even to their pets.

BEAN THERE

Here's a quick phone quiz. Are you old enough to remember bag phones (the early generation of mobile phones)? How about renting your landline phone from the telephone company? Do you remember rotary-dial telephones? And here's a question you might not want to answer out loud, if you're as old as I am: do you remember party lines?

I'll never forget my first cell phone, which I purchased shortly after the first commercial cell phones hit the market in 1984. There is the leading edge of technology, and there is the bleeding edge of technology. I was on the bleeding edge. My first cell phone cost nine hundred sixty dollars. It was so big it came in a body bag. When you took your bag phone to lunch, you had to find a special chair to put it on. It was too big to sit on the table. My kids shake their heads in disbelief when I tell them this.

Cellular and digital technology have accomplished far more than simply shrinking the old bag phones to communication devices that are smaller than a deck of cards. The technology has introduced an entirely new cultural dynamic to the world and to human relationships. The impact of this technology on our social lives, habits, and lifestyles is hard to overestimate. We are becoming more spontaneous, more independent, more willing to share our personal lives in public. Cell phones are decreasing the boundaries between work and play, just as they increase our skills at multitasking. Cell phones are redefining and reinventing our relationships. They give us new ways to create social networks. They also have become our digital watches and wallets.

And there is more: Who could have predicted that cell phones would save the music industry? Who predicted cell phones would be our preferred computing devices?

COFFEE, THREE DOLLARS—CONNECTION, PRICELESS

Take out your cell phone and set it next to your cup of Starbucks. How much did your current cell phone cost you?

Chances are, it cost you nothing. That's because cell phone companies aren't selling cell phones. They're selling relationships. If you don't think your cell phone provider is selling relationships, try and get out of your contracted "relationship." You almost have to hire a divorce lawyer. We now have cell phone relationships that last far longer than many marriages.

Coffee, like your cell phone, goes with conversation. Conversation leads to connection. And connection is what we all hunger and thirst for. We literally can't live without it. And to get it, we're willing to stand in line and pay high prices. Ralph Waldo Emerson is alleged to have said that he would gladly walk a hundred miles through a snowstorm for one good conversation.

We establish the value of buying a product at Starbucks by our uncompromising quality and by building a personal relationship with each customer.

—HOWARD SCHULTZ[12]

All it takes today is a walk to your neighborhood Starbucks.

Starbucks is fundamentally in the relationship business. Starbucks sells not coffee but connection. In fact, anyone who is selling anything anymore isn't selling a product, but the experience of a relationship. That's why it's not enough for a Starbucks barista to know your name. They want to know your favorite brew first, and then your story. Then your name.

Forget *Cheers* ("where everybody knows your name"). Remember Starbucks ("where everybody wants to know your soul").

FRONT-PORCH CONNECTIONS

As we read the Starbucks cup, once again it brings us back to the gospel. The gospel of connection is the gospel of relationship, and the gospel of relationship leads us ultimately to God.

We have mentioned before that the EPIC life is nothing short of grande-passion spirituality, which is rich in faith and in intimacy with God. We hunger to connect with others because that's the way God designed us. At the same time, we can't help but hunger for God—whether we are aware of it or not—because only in God can we find completion.

Jesus was not a coffee drinker, but he was a master of connection. In fact, he was *the* master of connection. In the next chapter we'll watch as Jesus brings the EPIC life full circle, from an earthly experience of spiritual clarity to the eternal connection that brings joy and juice to your soul.

Ten

The Gospel
in a Connective Cup

Connecting Like St. Arbucks

The only ones who are afraid are
those who think they are alone.
—SAINT CATHERINE OF SIENA[1]

The business world has a new Golden Rule. It is the one statistic that increasingly is taken most seriously by investors, and it may be the one mark of success in the future that all companies will be required by law to report.[2]

When it was first developed by Fred Reichheld, loyalty expert and author, he called it the Net Promoter Score or NPS. It could also be called the Customer Evangelism Score.[3] It's not an eternal question; it has to do with temporal matters, yet it reveals everything about the future of a company, or a church, on earth.

So what is this measure of success? Every church, every Christian, and every business should seek the answer to this question: would you recommend us to a friend?[4]

The genius of this simple, seven-word question is that it assesses the number one asset any company or church can have: the grande passion that leads to brand loyalty. If the answer is no, and you hear that answer too frequently, you're probably in trouble. In fact, the Customer Evangelism Score quantifies a company's, or a church's, future success after subtracting the answers of "no" and "don't know" from the "yes" answers.

Two companies are legendary for their customer loyalty: Starbucks and American Express. Passionate loyalty is the only thing that can explain why some people won't frequent businesses that don't honor American Express cards. Or why some Starbucks fans like to "collect" as many Starbucks stores as possible.

As we have said already, Starbucks is a gathering place, a third place that people seek out without even realizing it. Starbucks is a coffee franchise that is invested in building community. That's one reason some of my friends and I refer to it as St. Arbucks.

But I have other friends who wear T-shirts with very different messages: one about not letting your friends drink Starbucks and another where the word *Starbucks* appears with one letter crossed out and replaced by another.

> *Starbucks is less about coffee and more about community.*
>
> —MARKET RESEARCHER
> WENDY LIEBMANN[5]

Starbucks is either passionately loved or hated. Why? If you are going to profess to be a third place, you'd better act like a third place. And this is where Starbucks is vulnerable. Go ahead: see what happens when you start treating Starbucks like your home away from home. Become a real porch sitter and test the reality against the rhetoric. See how friendly the baristas get when you bring in a crew to videotape your Bible-study group hanging out at a Starbucks. Or find out how hospitable the management becomes when you go through official channels trying to obtain permission to use a Starbucks's location to telecast a conversation about Starbucks and spirituality for a book that's being written. Suddenly fears about protecting the brand flair up from behind closed doors and turn baristas into bodyguards and wrangling bureaucrats.

But before we get on that high horse, remember how protective the church can be about its own image when local groups ask permission to use the facility for one function or another. Listen to how quickly the conversation gravitates away from hospitality to warding off all intruders who might advocate conflicting core values and mission statements.

BREWED FOR THOUGHT

Where do you most often experience dropped calls? What is the most ridiculous thing you have done to avoid a bad connection? I heard about a woman who used to lean out an upstairs window just to get a cell phone connection in her home. We're all willing to go out of our way for a good connection.

Back in the nineties, you couldn't enter certain Starbucks in downtown Seattle and Portland without wading through a mob of sign-wielding protesters. For a few years, picketing Starbucks was synonymous with protecting the environment and promoting global human rights. Today the same people continue to ring these downtown Starbucks, but from the inside. Starbucks now appears to be their home base—their meeting point and launching pad. What was once a battleground is now a rallying point. Can the church take a humble, redemptive lesson from Starbucks's success in turning placard-waving critics into card-carrying customers?

The community we hunger for—but which eludes many of us—needs as many proponents as it can get. In the past, the church was a third place of the highest order. Churches doubled as community centers, town meeting halls, centers for disseminating news, places of community celebration, and bases of operation during times of emergency. Churches saw themselves as much more than simply a place for members to gather on Sunday morning. In many small towns across the country, this is still largely the case. But for the most part, the church has lost its reputation for supporting and building community. I'm not against finding community wherever I can, in a coffee shop or elsewhere, but I look forward to the day that Christians and the church reclaim the identity of community builder.

WHY CONNECTION SELLS

The reason why Starbucks generates such loyalty in the land of brandscapes has less to do with the virtues of its coffee than its social virtues. Starbucks offers an essential third place where people can weave webs of connectedness. This keeps people coming back because we are disconnected. Take cell phone service. Cell phones and bad connections go together like Dr. Jekyll and Mr. Hyde. In fact, I get more bad connections on cell phones in urban areas of USAmerica (the most densely populated state, New Jersey, is notorious for dropped calls) than in remote game farms of South Africa, the freeways of South Korea, and the meandering byways of New Zealand.

> *Connections are rocks among the quicksands. The only permanent thing in your life is your connections.*
>
> —ZYGMUNT BAUMAN[6]

Bad connections ruin cell phone conversations, which is an irritation but not a tragedy. The tragedy is that bad connections ruin relationships and lives. There is good reason that EPIC ends with C: **C**onnective. Success, wealth, convenience, the world's highest standard of living. All of these add up to poverty if you're disconnected.

Maybe there's a reason why the question "Can you hear me now?" is heard loudest in the nation where consumerism has reached its highest peaks and exacted its worst tolls. We've traded relationships for refrigerators, cars, and other inanimate objects. We've traded relations for elations, community for commodity. Technology isolates us at the same time it connects us, thereby stimulating in us a hunger for the very thing it deprives us of. The most successful businesses are the ones you would recommend to a friend. It's almost impossible to *over*estimate the value of connection.

GROUNDS FOR TRUTH

As much as we long for connection, our culture still misses the point. Check out www.realtor.com. Here (under More Search Options) you will find boxes to click for what you want in your next home: Two bathrooms or three and a half? Two bedrooms or five? But how about a sidewalk or a front porch? Sorry, there is no box for sidewalk or for front porch either. Realtors don't even think about sidewalks or front porches as being of equal significance to garages, family rooms, and decks.

Why do expensive new homes have media rooms where a family can watch a movie in a minitheater setting, but the family never sees anyone they know at the video rental store? Why do homes now come with roomy, elaborate decks on the backs of the houses, but most with no front porches? Why does one in four households in Britain no longer possess a dinner table for a family to share meals? Sociologists are of one mind on this: the average person now has fewer friends. When compared to as recently as the 1980s, USAmericans have fewer relationships and less intimate friendships outside the family than they used to. That's one reason family members are becoming more important, and outside friends less so. That's also the big reason for the burgeoning relationship industries of counselors, coaches, therapists, trainers...a flotilla of "paid friends."

THE MINISTRY OF CONNECTION

In this culture of bad connections, Starbucks invited customers to "come here and connect." And that is how Starbucks built up a following of devoted patrons. If the church had known what business it was really in (the connection business), it would have said to this culture: "Let us be your front porch." But the church has divested itself of the connection business in order to master the principle business, the proposition business, and the being-right business. Its school of thought is now a school of ought. The church is by and large no longer in the relationship business.

If the truth of opera is the music, the truth of Christianity is the relationships. Just how far the church has wandered from that truth became apparent in 2000 when I was speaking at a church called the Meeting Place

GROUNDS FOR TRUTH

Here's an easy experiment you can do to test people's hunger for connectedness. Go to a movie matinee and arrive early. Chances are you'll be the first ones in the theatre. Find a seat, then watch what happens when other people arrive. Do they sit as far away from you as possible, or do they sit in the same part of the theatre where you're seated?

in downtown Winnipeg. When our morning coffee break began to take over the event, Tim Thiessen started a tug of war. He took the mike and called us back into the sanctuary. Tim Hortons coffee and doughnuts tugged back. Our leader then yanked us back into the sanctuary with, "Bring your coffee and doughnuts with you." Our hesitation jerked back. Then Tim pulled us over the line and won the contest with just one statement: "Bring your coffee and doughnuts, and add your stain to everyone else's."

I couldn't believe my ears. Here was the first church I had been in where the carpet was involved in ministry. In every other church, the ministry existed for the carpet. Whatever else happened, the carpet had to be kept clean. Here was a church where the most important thing was relationships. The Meeting Place was a space for relationships to develop and deepen. Relationships are messy, but so what if the carpet gets dirty? It can get cleaned, and when it can't get cleaned any longer, it can be replaced. The carpet exists for the ministry.

ONLY CONNECT

Two of the most widely quoted, deeply resonant words written in the second half of the twentieth century were originally hidden on the title page of novelist E. M. Forster's *Howards End:* "Only connect."[7]

The power of the epigraph even got the book listed as a religious tract. The Register Office in Cambridge, England, held that it was inappropriate to read from certain sacred or religious texts in civil marriage ceremonies in England and Wales. Mentioned in particular were readings from "the Bible, the Koran, the Torah, the Prophet (by Kahil [sic] Gibran) and Howard's [sic] End." E. M. Forster has written the only novel named by the registrar general in England as a religious tract.[8]

The key to the power of these words, *only connect,* is their oxymoronic double ring. The "only" me and the "connecting" we are not mutually exclusive, but mutually embracing. The sciences of chaos and nonequilibrium physics are based on the alienating forces of uncertainty and unpredictability while at the same time knowing that underlying everything that exists are fundamental embracing forces of interconnectedness, purposefulness, and endless possibilities. In other words, "if only" we can "connect," how different this world would be. The future belongs to the connectors, to those who can help people connect the lone and lonely dots of their lives and their world so that the big picture of wholeness and holiness can emerge. The gospel of Jesus Christ creates disciples with a two-word mission statement: "Only Connect."

LIFE'S FOUR BAD CONNECTIONS

The number one source of stress in life is the feeling of isolation—isolation from God, from yourself, from others, and from creation. In fact, Esther de Waal finds each of these bad connections in the original Adam and Eve garden story. Yet saving us from despair is the truth that Jesus, the Second Adam, came to heal these broken relationships. And by so doing, he restores us to the Garden.[9]

BREWED FOR THOUGHT

Think about life's four bad connections: our broken relationships with God, others, self, and creation. Which of these bad connections are you struggling with the most? What troubles you most about this bad connection?

Adam and Eve hid from the God who looked for them when they didn't show up for their daily walk. In their hiding we find the root of our broken relationship with God. They hid their nakedness with clothing, even though no one else was around. This is the root of each person's broken relationship with oneself. In their blaming of each other and the serpent for their disobedience, we find the root of our broken relationships with others. And finally, in the banishment from Eden, there is the root of our broken relationship with creation. Hence, Adam and Eve show us the four bad connections that dog our lives.

Paul gave the Christians living in Colossae the key to restoring bad connections. "In Christ all things cohere," he wrote.[10] Only Christ's healing power returns us to God, to each other, to ourselves, and to creation. In Christ all things connect, but how are the connections restored?

"Only Connect" with God

There is no greater challenge than to talk about God. We can talk about God only in language that comes from our creatureliness, and that explains why words fail us. God is beyond creatureliness, beyond the categories of the world and culture.

Still, words can begin to orient us toward God. If there is one thing we can say about God with absolute confidence, it is that the Maker of the Universe wants to have relationships with us. You hear this in the story of Adam and Eve. You hear it as well in the story of Abraham, when the Lord reminds Abraham: "I am your shield, your very great reward."[11] In other words, the blessing of a covenant relationship with God is not found in the benefits of the

> *God is sheer joy, and sheer joy demands companionship.*
> —SAINT THOMAS AQUINAS

relationship. The blessing *is* the relationship. You also hear this in the story of Jesus, who in the gospels prays twenty-one original prayers. Every one of them begins by addressing God as Father, a name drawn from human relationships.

No writer has expressed this better than C. S. Lewis, who pictures Satan presiding over a meeting of all of hell's lesser devils in *The Screwtape Letters*. Satan is instructing his minions about what they are up against in trying to defeat God's will for these despicable human creatures. Here Bishop William Willimon sums up Satan's instruction:

> Remember, disgusting as it may seem to you, God really loves those weak, filthy human vermin that crawl the earth.... He really wants them finally happy.... That's why he's so mysterious with them. He wants something more than mere obedience. His master plan is to win from them the free, unforced recognition of his love, and the free, unforced response to it.[12]

Some people have food allergies. I have word allergies. I break out in hives every time I hear the phrase *intelligent design*. The God of Adam and Eve, Abraham and Sarah, the Father God of Jesus, is so much more than an Intelligent Designer. God is an Extravagant Lover, an All-Consuming Incandescence who says to every one of us, "For better or for worse, I make this covenant with you." No matter how much we try to forget about God, and however much we may succeed, we can count on one thing: God will *not* forget about us. No matter how broken and battered our relationship with God, God keeps God's promises. We may not keep promises, but God does.

But if the phrase *intelligent design* gives me hives, *servant* language sends me into anaphylactic shock. Jesus didn't christen us servants. He chose to call

BREWED FOR THOUGHT

It's no secret that words are limited, but when we describe someone, words are the tools we have at hand. What words come to mind first when you think about God? Write them down, and then contemplate how those words begin to open your heart to who God is.

us friends.[13] Usually there is a halo effect over anyone's last words, so you'd think the church would listen especially hard to Jesus' final instructions. He had to choose his concluding words carefully. And he chose to say this: God wants a relationship with you, not as servants, but as friends. "I no longer call you servants.... Instead, I have called you friends."[14] John Wesley's Aldersgate experience was his transformation from being God's servant to being God's friend.

> *I see myself as a classic. I never loved another person as I loved myself.*
>
> —MAE WEST at seventy-eight[15]

Jesus' final directive is not a work assignment: "Serve." Jesus' final directive is a renaming embrace: "Friends."[16] Think of it: the Savior of the world wants me not to be his servant but to be his friend, even his child.

"Only Connect" with Self

Each one of us is an original work of divine art. God's artwork is made up of three elements: body, spirit, soul. There is a role for each element, and each element needs to hold together and connect with the other elements. They are each one-of-a-kind, original elements that too often get disconnected: fragmented and faceted in the confusing desires of standing out and fitting in.

The essence of art is "making special."[17] God made each one of us special, but consider how quickly we get separated from our specialness. The biblical language for making special is "holiness," or "set apart." For example, God declares to Jeremiah that even as he is known he has also been "set apart"—*hiqdis.* From the Hebrew root *qds,* this

> *Fashion can be defined as one who wants to stand out being imitated by many who don't.*
>
> —PAUL VALÉRY

verb indicates the act of setting something apart for a unique, specific reason or use. In religious usage this meant setting something aside as special to Yahweh—that is, holy or consecrated. Once this special designation was made, that which was set apart was only for Yahweh's use. Thus, according to Jeremiah's calling, he is for God's use—and God alone. The biblical call to holiness is a relational mandate that requires the connecting of the body, spirit, and soul that God has specially made and made special.

Brewed for Thought

Take a few moments to think about yourself. What words come to mind that describe who you are? What is your specialness—the things that set you apart for God's use?

It is interesting to see the difference between medieval jewelry and modern jewelry. Medieval jewels were not faceted. That custom was introduced during the Renaissance. In contrast, medieval jewels were rounded and polished so as to give an inner illumination and impression of light glowing from within. It's time to start polishing again. We are not art for art's sake, but art for God's sake: *ars gratia Dei*.

"Only Connect" with Others

"We worked together in the same town." Notice what that means: it's another way of saying that we never once shared a meal together while we were there and we never once made an effort to get together.

> *Mankind is one body. We cannot move forward except together. We cannot leave parts of our body behind. None of us is free until we all are free.*
>
> —James Mawdsley[18]

Our precaffeinated ancestors had a communal spirit: fellowship and festivity were fostered within religious communities. Using a favorite metaphor of the Bible to explain the interweaving of humans together, church and community knit people together.[19] But modern Christianity lost that knitting. It unraveled the threads and dismantled the bonding agents to the point where Western culture is now becoming floating islands of "singletons."

A research report was prepared by Dartmouth Medical School and others to discover the causes for children becoming at risk. The report hoped to "spark a much needed conversation on how we can better help our children grow up healthy, whole and ready for a productive and happy life."[20] The report's conclusions are significant, finding that humans are hardwired to form relationships:

- Early nurture powerfully affects brain development.
- Nurture can neutralize genetic vulnerabilities.
- The biologically based need for nurture continues through adolescence.
- Human beings are biologically primed to seek moral and spiritual meaning, and nurturing relationships are a central foundation for positive moral and spiritual development.
- Nurturing relationships and a spiritual connection to the transcendent significantly improve physical and emotional health.[21]

BREWED FOR THOUGHT

The importance of nurture and relationship can't be overstated. Think about your best friend. What attracts you to your friend? How are you similar, and how do you differ? What do you value most about this friendship? What is most challenging about this friendship?

The commission also found that humans need authoritative communities throughout their lifetimes. The commission coined the term *authoritative communities*[22] because social science had "no name for the set of institutions that play this nurturing role. This namelessness is highly significant: These institutions have no name because social science hasn't recognized the critical importance of their role."[23]

> *This culture, which replaces community with management, stories with curriculum, and care with commodities, is the serviced society—a careless place dominated by impotent institutions and burgeoning social pathology.*
>
> —NORTHWESTERN UNIVERSITY
> PROFESSOR JOHN MCKNIGHT [24]

Faith communities can be the best embodiments of authoritative communities. The ten key characteristics of authoritative communities have been weakened severely by a wide range of social forces in recent decades.[25] In the absence of faith communities functioning as authoritative communities, people are both floating adrift by themselves and looking for lifeboats.

In the Bible, there is no such thing as a self-contained self, only a relational self, a connected self. If you're "in Adam," you are home alone. If you're "in Christ," you are home together. You are in *koinonia*.

> *Freedom is indivisible; the chains on any one of my people were the chains on all of them, the chains on all of my people were the chains on me.*
>
> —NELSON MANDELA[26]

In our shrinking world, we can be linked by acquaintance to anyone in the world in six steps. Only very few random connections are needed between clusters of local connections to facilitate a small world system. It's the randomization that brings the blessing, or the curse. The Black Death was devastating because rats randomized the connections, passing the disease more rapidly than human contact alone. But the opposite works as well. Positive randomization of connections that are good and true can bring amazing results.

Robert Putnam has suggested a valuable distinction between groups that are bridging and those that are bonding. As examples of the first, he cites civil rights movements, youth service groups, or ecumenical religious organizations; of the second, ethnic fraternal organizations, fashionable country clubs, or church-based groups.[27] This distinction between bonding and bridging is present in the Last Supper, where Jesus' words used in blessing the bread and the cup betray a distinction in distribution, a distinction so slight and subtle it is often overlooked.

The bread is offered to the disciples: "And as they were eating, Jesus took bread, blessed and broke it, and gave it to them and said, 'Take it; this is my body.' "[28] But note what words Jesus uses when he lifted up the cup: "This is my blood of the covenant, which is poured out for many."[29]

The bread is for the bonding of those in the Upper Room. The cup is for the bridging to "the many," or as it is translated in most Eucharistic prayers, "all." The new covenant honors both bonding and bridging. The bread is "for you." The cup is "for you and for many."[31] Jesus

> *We are members one of another.*
> —SAINT PAUL[30]

proclaimed peace to those "who were far off" and those "who were near."[32] Churches need to become as adept at bridging (symbolized by Paul) as they can be at bonding (symbolized by Peter). Christians don't believe in burning bridges, only building them by speaking and listening in ways that bond.

"Only Connect" with Creation

Only a few people don't have a sense of humor. But untold numbers of people don't have a sense of place. And like an absent sense of humor, you know when a sense of place is missing. Just look around you, and the loss of connection with the earth is obvious in everything from godforsaken strip malls to the raunch culture of ranch suburbia.

For Christians, there was no Holy Land before Jesus. Israel became the

Holy Land for Christians because of the way Jesus lived and loved. He made the land holy. We too can make our locale holy by the way we live and love, beginning with the way we view our relationship to creation.

What if we were to see the things in our locale less as commodities and more as connections? Take trees. In India there is a poetic phrase for "the forest culture": *aranyi sanskriti.* In aranyi sanskriti trees are not viewed as a resource or in terms of a quantifiable commodity, but as a source of our connectedness to air, light, food, water, and beauty. The connection is not hard to demonstrate. For example, humans inhale oxygen and exhale carbon dioxide, while trees do just the opposite. Trees and other plants process water, carbon dioxide, sunlight, and other elements through photosynthesis. In the process, plants release oxygen. It would be difficult to imagine a closer connection than our relationship to plant life that produces the gas we depend on for human life.

In biblical Hebrew there is no word for nature, because nature is not something separate from us. We are a part of it, and it is a part of us.[33] "Only connect" is the basis for conserving and caring for creation.

RELATIONAL CODES OF CONDUCT

One of the original meanings of the Latin *conversari,* from which we get our word *conversation,* was "to live together." The EPIC life empowers us to live together, and EPIC codes enable us to live together well. What codes do you live by so that we all can live together?

Technology reduces everything to binary codes of zero and one.

Politics reduces everything to legal codes of legislation.

Religions reduce everything to moral codes of principles.

Jesus reduced everything to a one-word relational code: love.

What is life without a grande passion? It is existence perhaps. It is respiration, circulation, digestion. It is a matter of taking up space and using up resources. But without grande passion and the connection of shared passions, life doesn't truly qualify as life.

We can't help but seek life on an EPIC scale, because God designed us that way. The life God desires for us is experiential, participatory, image-rich, and connective. The life of faith, to fully qualify as a *life* of faith, is characterized by experiences that are meaningful; full participation in those experiences of meaning; a richness of imagery wrapped around those experiences; and deep connections with God, others, self, and creation. All four EPIC elements, enlivened and intertwined, deliver grande passion, the life we're all thirsty for.

Don't wait until next week. Don't cheat yourself out of another moment of the EPIC life. Go ahead and treat yourself, and a friend, to your favorite cup o' joe. Meet at Starbucks, or your favorite gathering place, and spend time experiencing the sights and sounds, enjoying the taste and aroma, relaxing in the warmth and connection of the EPIC life. I'll be ordering a black eye. I'll leave your order up to you.

The main thing is this: don't delay. Why put off grande passion when it's right there within your reach?

Epilogue

Jehovah Java

Espresso is a miracle of chemistry in a cup.
—ILLYCAFFÈ FOUNDER ANDREA ILLY[1]

*I*f you *still* doubt the religious and spiritual significance of coffee, read this quick history of java. Historians have credited the rise of the coffee culture in Europe with everything from the birth of modernity and the crucible of the Enlightenment, to the decline of alcohol dependence, to the birth of civil discourse and the art of conversation. And that's not all. Some historians credit coffee as the fuel of the Protestant work ethic and the alliance of coffee and print as a significant component of the Protestant Reformation itself. For more amazing coffee facts, history, and legends, read on.

COFFEE: A QUICK HISTORY

Starbucks is a USAmerican version of a Chinese discovery first chewed by the Ethiopians then brewed by the Arabs then commercialized by the Egyptians and Syrians and later cultivated into an art form by the Italians. Here's a quick CliffsNotes history of what's in your coffee cup:

The Chinese first discovered caffeine in 2737 BC (improvable but legendary) and used it as medicinal tea.[2] The Ethiopians took raw beans that grew in the highlands and either masticated them or brewed the leaves like tea.

When the "black and comely"[3] Ethiopian Queen Makeda, whom we know as the Queen of Sheba, paid a visit to King Solomon in Jerusalem and posed hard questions, she first plied him with precious spices—among them frankincense, myrrh,[4] and (some say) coffee beans.

If the first use of coffee was medicinal, its second use was spiritual, as Sufi mystics figured out how to extract the "wine of the bean" by brewing coffee. This enhanced their spiritual awareness, fortified rituals of ecstatic dance, and sustained all-night spinning ceremonies popular among those that Westerners dubbed "whirling dervishes."

Coffee began as the Muslim alternative to alcohol, and by the fifteenth century, the "wine of Islam" had spread throughout the Islamic world. "Muslim wine" also made many Arabs fabulously wealthy, especially those in the port city of al-Makkha (hence "mocha"), where the business of brewing arabica coffee beans had started around 1200 CE and where merchants from around the world girdled the city and gridlocked the harbor.

The Egyptians and Syrians started the coffeehouse tradition in the sixteenth century. In the late sixteenth and early seventeenth centuries, Venetian merchants brought coffee beans to Europe, and a Dutch trader brought a coffee plant. By 1650, when a Lebanese man named Jacob set up Western Europe's first coffeehouse at the college town of Oxford, coffeehouses started spreading throughout Europe. Tea was a private drink and a woman's drink; coffee was a public drink and a man's drink. Even when a fifth of London coffeehouses were presided over by women owners or proprietors, coffeehouses themselves were a masculine environment where socially diverse customers could set aside their differences of rank and station to engage in common conversation about the news of the day being circulated in new forms of print media.

NECTAR OF THE GODS

From its premodern beginnings, coffee was freighted with religious, social, and medicinal significance. Every religion has its sacred libation: Christians and Jews, wine; Buddhists, tea; Hindus, milk (from sacred cows). The Muslim sacred drink was coffee. According to legend, the Italian Pope Clement VIII (1592–1605) was pressured to ban coffee as an insidious threat from Muslim Turkey, but after insisting on tasting it before issuing the prohibition, the pope baptized it as a Christian drink.

Initially, coffee was consumed only as part of a religious ceremony or on the advice of a physician. When, as a child, Robert Louis Stevenson (1850–1894) couldn't sleep, his nurse-nanny "Cummy" would give him cups of strong black coffee to drink. The religious connection to coffee is made explicit in certain languages. In Norwegian, the word for coffee "bean" is the same as the word for "prayer."[5] This connection between coffee and faith became even more apparent in the modern era, when coffee became the beverage of modernity and Protestantism. Coffee culture made it possible for the Protestant Reformation to shake Europe out of its beer-besotted somnambulance, and coffee fueled the Protestant work ethic. Some historians have even argued that the spread of both Protestantism and capitalism were lubricated by the drink of coffee.[6] "The modern world was washed into existence on the tide of caffeine," writes Steven Shapin.[7]

Coffee was the beverage of industry, initiative, and integrity—the antithesis of alcohol. It would sober you up, stimulate mental and physical activity, and get you thinking straight and living right. Alcoholic drinks made you dizzy and fuzzy and dull; coffee made you sober and serious and smart.

Heightened perception rather than inebriated dullness was "black wine's" badge of distinction, its Protestant branding. Coffee was, as one scholar puts it, "the ideal beverage, in short, for the Age of Reason."[8]

It would be hard to underestimate the alcoholic grip that held Europe in bondage during the Dark Ages. Safer to drink than water, alcohol was consumed at extremely high levels through the Middle Ages and beyond. The average beer consumption in Northern Europe and Puritan New England in the seventeenth century has been estimated to be six to eight pints a day, or the equivalent of almost two six-packs a day, but with higher alcoholic content.[10] That figure includes women and children.[11]

> *[Coffee] spread through the body and achieved chemically and pharmacologically what rationalism and the Protestant ethic sought to fulfill spiritually and ideologically.*
>
> —HISTORIAN
> WOLFGANG SCHIVELBUSCH[9]

And the upper classes drank more. "Finnish soldiers were given a ration of five liters of strong ale a day" (that's our alcoholic equivalent of forty cans a day). Monks in England had to make do with twelve cans per day.[12]

In a world where almost every child born had some form of fetal alcohol syndrome, the cultural impact of coffee is almost inconceivable. "Within two hundred years of Europe's first cup," one historian has noted, "famine and the plague were historical footnotes. Governments became more democratic, slavery vanished, and the standards of living and literacy went through the roof."[13] Or to hear the more contemporary sounds of one anonymous English Puritan in a poem from 1674:

When the sweet Poison of the Treacherous Grape
Had acted on the world a general rape;
Drowning our Reason and our souls
In such deep seas of large o'erflowing bowls....

When foggy Ale, leavying up mighty trains,
Of muddy vapours, had besieg'd our Brains,
Then Heaven in Pity…,
First sent amongst us this All-healing Berry.…

Coffee arrives, that grave and wholesome Liquor,
That heals the stomach, makes the genius quicker,
Relieves the memory, revives the sad,
And cheers the Spirits, without making mad.[14]

INFORMATION BROKERED BY COFFEE

It took a while for coffee to catch on in all of Europe. Until the seventeenth century, coffee was a curiosity for most Europeans. But coffeehouses started spreading throughout Europe around 1650, presenting a radical alternative to ale-soaked pubs. Unlike the squalor, darkness, and dirtiness of taverns, coffeehouses were well lighted, full of bookshelves, mirrors, quality furniture, and art work. In aristocratic circles, the form in which coffee was served became paramount. It mattered what kind of porcelain was used. In more bourgeois circles, what mattered was the content more than the form: what did it taste like?

In a Christmas special on how coffee fueled the information world of the seventeenth and eighteenth centuries, *The Economist* called coffee "the Internet in a cup."[15] Coffeehouses were "information exchanges" for movers and shakers. "Collectively, Europe's interconnected web of coffee-houses formed the Internet of the Enlightenment era."[16] One historian has noted the historical convergence of the coffeehouse and the commodification of news: "Coffee was urban, public, radical, egalitarian. Alert coffee drinkers, their brains unfuddled by alcohol, read the papers and pamphlets and discussed what they read. 'What news?' was a customary greeting upon entering a coffee house, and supposedly coffee drinkers discoursed without any concern for distinction of rank."[17]

Such an egalitarian sharing of information rankled the authorities to the point where, in 1675, Charles II issued a proclamation banning coffeehouses. His spies had reported: "The common people talke anything, for every carman and porter is now a statesman; and indeed the coffee houses are good for nothing else."[18] Since men were spending so much time in all-male coffeehouses, and coffee was seen to be an anti-erotic drink, "the whole race was in danger of extinction" argued "The Women's Petition Against Coffee, representing to public consideration the Grand inconveniences accruing to their sex from the excessive use of the drying and enfeebling Liquor."[19]

Coffeehouses were incubators of modernity: their patrons were the leaders of the Enlightenment in science, education, literature, commerce, and politics. And each coffeehouse had a brand name that advertised its specialty: one for philosophers, one for writers, one for businessmen, one for poets. At Will's aspiring writers hung out. At the Child's coffeehouse, clergy debated theology. In London, coffeehouses around St. Paul's Cathedral were thronged by clergy and theologians who were known for their milky white coffee which some called derisively "the lactification of the coffee-house."

The more coffee prospered, the more conversation as an art began to flourish until the eighteenth century became known as "the Age of Conversation."[20] In coffeehouse discourse, a *gentleman* was defined as a "man of conversation,"[21] and the gift of seductive persuasion, or "talking people round," became the ideal of rational discourse. It was all very civilized and clearheaded: if you started a quarrel at a coffeehouse, you had to atone for it by buying a round of coffee for all those present.

Discussion Guide

Questions for Coaching and Conversation

by Edward Hammett

*U*se the following questions to help you explore practical ways to live with grande passion. The questions are designed to prompt both personal reflection and great discussions with friends, and are also useful for life coaching. Additional questions inspired by *The Gospel According to Starbucks* and designed for reflection, discussion, and coaching can be found at www .leonardsweet.com, www.transformingsolutions.org, and www.thecolumbia partnership.org.

INTRODUCTION: THE BREW OF THE SOUL

The questions in this guide are written to stir the BREW, an acronym that stands for Being Real Engages the World. As you pursue a life of grande passion and EPIC faith, reflect on the personal meaning behind each word (Being Real Engages the World).

Being

Think about what it means to grow fully into the person God made you to be.

1. Who do you want to be now?
2. What is creating who you are?
3. What distracts you from being all you can be?
4. What will move you from where you are to where God wants you to be?

Real

In being who God made you to be, think about what it means to be real.

5. How much of who you are now is who you *want* to be?
6. What is going on in you and through you that you are not proud of?
7. What would have to change in order for you to be more real?
8. What would make your life more pleasing to God?
9. What is the best version of yourself? How often do you see it?

Engages The

Think about the effect your life has.

10. What places in your daily life intersect with your life mission?
11. Who are the people in your path who fuel your life mission? Who are the ones who drain your life mission?
12. What do you want to do to achieve your life mission that you are not currently doing? What or who could help you do that right now?

World

Think about your life mission in terms of the people in your sphere of influence and the world that surrounds you.

13. How are you currently impacting the world you work in?
14. What impact are you having on your family? on your community?

15. Who specifically in your world needs encouragement, love, or hope?

16. Where does your greatest passion intersect with the world's greatest needs?

CHAPTER 1: READING A STARBUCKS CUP

1. How do you seek meaning and passion in your spiritual life? What practice(s) do you engage in regularly that nurture your soul, your dreams, and your passion?

2. Which relationships nurture your soul? Which relationships drain your soul and destroy its voice?

3. Consider the important things that are missing from your relationships. What can you do to recapture the aroma of fulfilling, soul-restoring relationships?

4. What can you do to stay connected with your soul, so that intellectual belief doesn't crowd out lived faith?

5. One person can change the world—for good or for ill. Where does the power-of-one factor show up in your life? How do you want to impact your family, friends, community, and world?

CHAPTER 2: LIFE ON AN EPIC SCALE

1. EPIC spirituality goes beyond mere belief to a consuming experience of God. What is present in your life that leaves you feeling incomplete or unfulfilled?

2. Take time to reflect on your life in light of the EPIC qualities of experience, participation, richness of images, and connection. In which area or areas are adjustments called for?

3. Do you believe God really does hammer trash cans into treasure chests? Why, or why not?

4. How have you seen God redeem areas of weakness in your life? How has God's work energized you and deepened your meaning?

Chapter 3: Drinking In the Starbucks Experience

1. Have you been living too much in your head to the neglect of your heart? If so, what do you sacrifice when you live in your head at the expense of your heart?
2. What are the things that help you *bring together* head and heart? How can you spend more time engaged with those things?
3. What is the return on investment (ROI) of your life investments? What shifts would make your life investments more fruit bearing and more fulfilling?
4. What are your most fulfilling life experiences? As you think about those experiences, how can you honor the values that will move you closer to your dreams and calling?

Chapter 4: The Gospel in an Experiential Cup

1. Simone Weil asked the question, "Can you love God without knowing him?" and answered in the affirmative. How would you answer this question? Why?
2. A life that is rich and deep in experience includes the experience of your *dislikes*. Do you agree that it's not until we discover why we don't like some things that we find out why we really like other things? Why or why not?
3. How does your life glorify God? What are the specifics that you can point to?
4. What is the evidence of the Creator's signature on your life? How do people see Christ in you?

CHAPTER 5: LIFE IS EMPTY UNTIL YOU JOIN IN

1. Who or what is calling you to deeper life experiences? What are the places and/or experiences that you want to jump into?
2. What in your life is void of meaning? What will help bring meaning and make your life more meaning filled?
3. What keeps you from participating in life—engaging more fully in your daily life at home, at work, and with friends?
4. Can you think of examples of how this is not a world of "I think, therefore I am" but "I choose, therefore I am?"[1] Give some examples of media campaigns that factor in high levels of interactivity.
5. Take a look at Web sites that offer "consumer" feedback to the church. Sites such as www.ChurchRater.com and www.church marketingsucks.com attempt to provide feedback through meaningful dialogue about the good, bad, and ugly of the church.

CHAPTER 6: THE GOSPEL IN A PARTICIPATORY CUP

1. What are the attachments in your life? Which of these attachments have a stronger hold than they should?
2. In keeping with the customized label of your coffee preference, how would you name the best version of yourself that honors the dreams and passions God has planted in your life? What would help you live into that dream?
3. According to IBM founder Thomas Watson Sr., "The fastest way to succeed is to double your failure rate." What are you doing to double your failure rate?
4. The greatest gift my mentor gave me was helping me learn to move through my fear and to embrace creativity and spontaneity. When I learned to trust God and act on the ideas, dreams, and passions he

placed in my heart, that's when my life and ministry took a new energizing and fruit-bearing direction. What would your life look like if you were no longer controlled by your fears of what others might think?

CHAPTER 7: BRANDS AS IMAGE STATEMENTS

1. Albert Einstein said, "Imagination is more important than knowledge." What do you do to nurture and act on your imagination? Who or what nurtures that side of your faith and dreams?
2. What are the signs in your life? What would happen if you paid attention to the signs you have been ignoring? If you created new signs, what would they say?
3. Whose voices do you pay attention to? What other voices do you need to listen to? What will help you now to listen to those voices?
4. What is a landmark or an icon that would describe your life now? What are the pictures or symbols that document your spiritual journey?

CHAPTER 8: THE GOSPEL IN AN IMAGE-RICH CUP

1. What makes a hero for you? How many of these hero characteristics do others see in you?
2. What image or symbol captures the essence of your calling, your biggest dream, and your experience of God?
3. How could this image or symbol be used to remind you of your commitment to the dream of moving forward in life and faith?
4. What decisions have you made so far while reading this book? What do you need to do now to honor these commitments?

Chapter 9: Your Undeniable Thirst for Connection

1. What are the sources of connection that you rely on most often? How are these sources working for you? What would make the connection more transforming and powerful?

2. As you consider the final aspect of the EPIC life, *connection*, think about the things that will help you remember an aroma of new dreams, new challenges, and new steps of faith. What are those triggers?

3. What questions do you need someone to ask you regularly to help you maintain your focus?

4. What is God's Spirit saying to you now? What is your response?

Chapter 10: The Gospel in a Connective Cup

1. Who are the biggest givers in your life? Now, rethink your answer. Is it possible that your life's biggest givers could be those who take most freely of your love? Why or why not?

2. Where are the bad connections in your life? In light of that, what new connections are needed?

3. How do you describe your relationship with God and his relationship with you? How would you characterize that connection?

4. Briefly describe your world, and as you do, listen for words and phrases that identify connections. Where are the roots of relationship that bring stability to your life? What entry points do you create for others to connect with you, and for you to connect with others?

Edward H. Hammett serves as senior coach and consultant for the Baptist State Convention of North Carolina and the Columbia Partnership. He works with a variety of churches and denominations as a coach, consultant, and conference leader, and is the author of several books, including *Spiritual Leadership in a Secular Age*.

Appendix A

Reason Versus Experience

How Reason Gained the Upper Hand in the Church

*C*hristianity hasn't always granted right belief the upper hand over a believer's authentic experience of God. In premodern times and in the Eastern church, religious experience was not held suspect in the laboratory of reason. But in the West, after the Enlightenment, rationalism and doctrine gained ascendancy.

In the modern West, Christianity was either a rational religion or another way of being rational. Very few (such as Jonathan Edwards) saw Christian faith as beyond rationality. Western Christianity sought the rationality of all being rather than the mystery of all being: it pursued the truth within human speech rather than the truth beyond human speech. The dominant tradition in modern Western thought has regarded emotion as a burden to human existence and an impediment to reason, the nucleus of human nature. How we acceptably expressed our emotions in the modern era without being thought a theological troglodyte was through music. Today we go to concerts and museums in the same spirit with which our ancestors went to church and went on pilgrimages.

In the modern world that is collapsing at our feet, we learned to trust experiments in a scientific laboratory more than experiences in the laboratory of life. An enormous shift in Western Christianity took place during the "Long Reformation" (1300–1700) that modernized and Protestantized Christianity. We went from privileging religious practice and religious experience to privileging religious belief and critical thought. The mind took ascendance over the soul and the spirit. Christianity became a "belief system," with a distinct worldview. Things once seen as religious were no longer found at the core of faith, things such as relationships, practices, embodiments, and experiences. The aim of premodern faith was union with God, and the path to that union was desire. But in the modern era, the longing that fed the divine pursuit and the emotion that drove it lost their religious cachet. Modern Christian faith was rational. The aim of modern faith was knowledge, especially scientific rationalist knowledge, and the path to knowledge was through the question. This explains why Christians in the West became more interested in beliefs about prayer than prayer experiences and practices. This also explains why the nation that most embodied Enlightenment values and rational culture became the nation of fascism and genocide.

Less Greek, More Geek and Hebrew

Eastern cultures have their own reasons to get on their knees. But at their best they retained the conjugation of reason and emotion through the integrative concept of *ki* (*kimochi* in Japanese, *kibun* in Chinese), which was defined not as "feelings" (which come and go) but as a structural feature of every human being.[1]

Perhaps it is time for Christianity's conversation partners to be other than Western: a case could be made for the Greco-Roman captivity of the church as much as for the Constantinian captivity of the church. In the prophetic words of theologian Amos Yong, it may be time to ask "what the gospel might look like if its primary dialogue partners are not Plato, Aristotle, Kant, Hegel, or Whitehead, but rather the Buddha, Confucius, Lao-tzu, Chuang-tzu, Nagarjuna, Shankara, Ramanuja, Chu Hsi, Dogen, Wang Yang Ming, and so on."[2] If the church can learn from Starbucks, why not from Star (Asian) TV? If Christianity really wanted to get radical, the first thing it could do would be to stop privileging Western rationalism.

Notes

Introduction

1. Carlos Fuentes, *This I Believe: An A to Z of a Life* (New York: Random House, 2005), 13.
2. Nick Reding, "Java Man," *Fast Company,* May 2006, 73, www.fast company.com/magazine/105/food-coffee.html (accessed 20 June 2006). For example, in 2006, 82 percent of adult USAmericans drank coffee, up from 79 percent in 2004. See also Jeffrey Kluger, "The Buzz on Caffeine," *Time,* 20 December 2004, 52.
3. Reding, "Java Man," 73. Sixteen billion pounds of coffee are grown annually worldwide. Latin America produced 70 percent of the world's coffee (Brazil alone accounts for one-third).
4. Starbucks says it has a "short" (eight fluid ounces). Ever see one?
5. Isak Dinesen, "The Supper at Elsinore," *Seven Gothic Tales* (New York: Harrison Smith and Robert Haas, 1934), 245.
6. *National Coffee Drinking Trends* (New York: National Coffee Association of the U.S.A., 2005), 10, 14, 24, 57. While the daily per capita consumption of coffee is 1.8 cups of coffee, coffee drinkers average 3.33 cups per day. In 2005, 26 percent of eighteen- to twenty-four-year-olds (an increase of 10 percentage points since 2003) drank coffee, and 16 percent downed gourmet coffee beverages daily. The figure was 33 percent for twenty-five to thirty-year-olds and 14 percent drinking gourmet coffee beverages.
7. Jackson Kuhl, "Tempest in a Coffeepot: Starbucks Invades the World," *Reason Online,* January 2003, www.readon.com/0301/cr.jk.tempest.shtml (accessed 14 June 2006). USAmericans consumed a little more than ten pounds of coffee per capita in 2000.

8. It's hard to beat Finland's per capita nine cups of coffee per day or twenty-four pounds of coffee beans per year.

9. ThinkExist.com, "Turkish Proverb Quotes," http://en.thinkexist.com/ quotation/coffee_should_be_black_as_hell-strong_as_death/168633 .html (accessed 17 June 2006).

10. For more on this, see the studies by Professor Joe Vinson of Scranton University, Pennsylvania, which canvassed USAmerica and Great Britain, and "Coffee 'Gives More Antioxidants than Fruit and Veg,' " 29 August 2005, www.telegraph.co.uk/news/main.jhtml?xml=/news/ 2005/08/29/wcoffee29.xml&sSheet=/news (accessed 6 October 2006). See also the research of Thomas Hofmann, professor and director of the Institute for Food Chemistry at the University of Muenster in Germany, cited in Veronika Somoza and others, "Activity-Guided Identification of a Chemopreventive Compound in Coffee Beverage Using in Vitro and in Vivo Techniques," *Journal of Agricultural and Food Chemistry* 51 (2003): 6861–69.

11. "Researchers are uncovering mechanisms by which a range of dietary agents—including coffee, wine, and cinnamon—appear to restore some of the body's responsiveness to insulin and control of blood sugar." Janet Raloff, "Coffee, Spices, Wine," *Science News* 165 (01 May 2004): 282. See also Jaakko Tuomilehto and others, "Coffee Consumption and Risk of Type 2 Diabetes Mellitus Among Middle-Aged Finnish Men and Women," *Journal of the American Medical Association* 291 (10 March 2004): 1213–19. This *JAMA* article was followed by Rob M. Van Dam and Frank B. Hu, "Coffee Consumption and Risk of Type 2 Diabetes: A Systematic Review," *Journal of the American Medical Association* 294 (6 July 2005): 97–104.

12. The Harvard School of Public Health conducted a study that found that male coffee drinkers who average four to five cups a day cut their risk of developing Parkinson's disease by nearly 50 percent. Further:

"Researchers in Germany found that methylpyridinium, a compound created during the coffee roasting process, may offer protection against colon cancer, and Brazilian scientists say caffeine might improve male fertility." *Trend Letter,* 24 April 2006, 6.

13. For more on this, also consider this source: Peter N. Witt, Charles F. Reed, and David B. Peakall, *A Spider's Web: Problems in Regulatory Biology* (New York: Springer Verlag, 1968), 61, which shows a picture of a web spun by a spider that wasn't on caffeine, then the picture of a web produced after the spider was under the influence of caffeine. To view a picture of the caffeinated web, see Silvia Helena Cardosa, "Behavioral Experiment: Drugged Spiders," *Mind and Behavior,* August 2001, www.cerebromente.org.br/n13/experiment/spider.htm (accessed 15 June 2006).

14. Leonard Sweet, *A Cup of Coffee at the SoulCafe* (Nashville: Broadman & Holman, 1998).

15. ThinkExist.com, "Turkish Proverb Quotes," http://en.thinkexist.com/ quotation/a_cup_of_coffee_commits_one_to_forty_years_of/328112 .html (accessed 13 June 2006).

16. Bruce Horovitz, "Starbucks Aims Beyond Lattes to Extend Brand," *USA Today,* 19 May 2006, A2, http://usatoday.com/money/industries/ food/2006-05-18-starbucks-usat_x.htm (accessed 6 October 2006).

17. John 10:10.

18. See Luke 16:8.

19. See Genesis 2:16.

20. See Revelation 22:17.

Chapter 1

1. Luke 16:8, KJV.

2. In 1999, Cold Stone Creamery CEO Doug Ducey had a goal to expand from seventy-four to one thousand ice cream stores by 2005.

It made that goal and became one of the twenty fastest-growing franchises in USAmerica. The growth was fueled by EPIC business practices. For more, go to the Cold Stone Creamery Web page: www.cold stonecreamery.com/main/index.asp (accessed 18 June 2006). See also Bruce Horowitz, "Ice Cream Shops Throw Sales with Scoops of Fun," *USA Today*, 9 June 2006, www.usatoday.com/money/industries/food/ 20060609icecreamusat_x.htm (accessed 18 June 2006). See also Jennifer Reingold and Ryan Underwood, "Was *Built to Last* Built to Last?" *Fast Company*, November 2004, 103, www.fastcompany.com/magazine/ 88/built-to-last.html (accessed 18 June 2006).

3. Stephen Moss, "The Gospel According to Ikea," *The Guardian*, 26 June 2000, www.guardian.co.uk/g2/story/0,3604,336379,00.html (accessed 14 May 2006).

4. Chad Hall, "NASCAR and the Emerging Culture," *CoolChurches: Resources for the Missional Church*, www.coolchurches.com/articles/ nascar.html (accessed 15 May 2006).

5. Jacques Derrida, *Of Grammatology*, trans. Gayatri Chakravorty Spivak (Baltimore, MD: The Johns Hopkins University Press, 1976), 158. Jacques Derrida's actual phrase is, "There is nothing outside of the text" (there is no outside text): *"Il n'y a pas de hors texte."*

6. So argues Jung Chang and Jon Halliday, *Mao: The Unknown Story* (New York: Knopf, 2005), 3.

7. Bruce Horovitz, "Starbucks Aims Beyond Lattes to Extend Brand," *USA Today*, 19 May 2006, A2, http://usatoday.com/money/industries/ food/2006-05-18-starbucks-usat_x.htm (accessed 6 October 2006).

8. IncoNet-Data Management report of October 2004, "IDM-AwalNet Team Up to Offer Wifi Internet Access at All Starbucks Outlets in Lebanon," www.idm.net.lb/about/news/2004/starbucks_wifi/index.asp (accessed 8 February 2005; 15 May 2006).

9. " 'Genius' Loves Java: Starbucks' Unique Collaboration with Ray
Charles Results in Eight Grammy Awards," CNNMoney.com, 14
February 2005, http://money.cnn.com/2005/02/14/news/fortune500/
starbucks_ray/index.htm (accessed 15 May 2006).

10. "Starbucks Entertainment and Liongate Announce a Partnership that
Transforms Traditional Motion Picture Marketing and Distribution
Model," *Forbes Business Wire*, 12 January 2006, www.forbes.com/
businesswire/feeds/businesswire/2006/01/12/busineswire2006011200
5278r1.html (accessed 15 May 2006). Starbucks's first foray into the
movie industry was *Akeelah and the Bee.*

11. "At Starbucks, a Blend of Coffee and Music Creates a Potent Mix," *The
Wall Street Journal*, 19 July 2005, A1.

12. James Citrin, director of Spencer Stuart, calls him the "chief evangelist
for Starbucks" in an interview on Lou Dobbs Tonight, aired 15 September 2004, CNN.com Transcripts, http://transcripts.cnn.com/
transcripts/0309/15/ldt.00.html (accessed 21 September 2006).

13. Bruce Sterling, *Mirrorshades: The Cyberpunk Anthology* (New York:
Arbor House, 1986), xiii. Reprinted in "Preface to *Mirrorshades*,"
http://project.cyberpunk.ru/idb/mirrorshades_preface.html (accessed
16 June 2006).

14. Kevin Kelly, *New Rules for the New Economy: 10 Radical Strategies for
a Connected World* (New York: Viking, 1998); Tom Peters writes, "If
you're not ready to be enterprise—and industry—reinvention evangelists, then.... Get out of your job," quoted in Regina Fazio Maruca,
"State of the New Economy," *Fast Company*, August 2000, 105,
www.fastcompany.com/magazine/38/one.html (accessed 18 June 2006);
Guy Kawasaki with Michele Moreno, *Rules for Revolutionaries: The
Capitalist Manifesto for Creating and Marketing New Products and Services* (New York: HarperBusiness, 1999); Jonathan Bulkeley, CEO of

BarnesandNoble.com, argues that "leaders today must be evangelists for changing the system—not for preserving it," quoted in Polly LaBarre, "Leaders.com: Unit of One," *Fast Company,* May 1999, 95, www.fastcompany.com/magazine/25/one.html (accessed 18 June 2006).

15. Benjamin Fulford, "The Web Phone Evangelist," *Forbes,* 13 December 1999, 69–74, www.forbes.com/forbes/1999/1213/6414068a.html (accessed 13 September 2006).

16. Maryanne Vollers, "Razing Appalachia," *Mother Jones,* July/August 1999, 38.

17. For John Bates, see "You Do What?" *Revolution,* July 2000, 11. For Karen Allen, see "Job Titles of the Future: Internet Evangelist," *Fast Company,* June 2000, 88, www.fastcompany.com/magazine/35/jtallen .html (accessed 18 June 2006).

18. Anna Muoio, "Should I Go.com?" Sidebar: "What's Your Web DNA?" *Fast Company,* July 2000, 170, www.fastcompany.com/magazine/36/ stein.html (accessed 18 June 2006).

19. "Jack Welch: Management Evangelist," *BusinessWeek,* 25 October 2004, 20, www.businessweek.com/magazine/content/04_43/b3905032 _mz072.htm (accessed 18 June 2006).

20. I borrow this phrase from Mari Sandoz, *Story Catcher* (Philadelphia: Westminster, 1963).

Chapter 2

1. Stephen Johnson, *Everything Bad Is Good For You: How Today's Popular Culture Is Actually Making Us Smarter* (New York: Riverhead, 2005).

2. I published sermons for nine years with www.homileticsonline.com and for five years with www.preachingplus.com. I currently publish with the first open-source preaching resource on the Web, www.wikiletics.com.

3. Chris Rubin, "Kopi Luwak: Wake Up and Smell the Coffee," *The Coffee Critic,* www.thecoffeecritic.com/fusion3/html/kopi.shtml (accessed

13 July 2006). See also Chris Brummitt, "Civet Coffee: Good to the Last Dropping," *USA Today,* 20 January 2004, www.usatoday.com/ news/offbeat/2004-01-20-civet-coffee_x.htm (accessed 13 July 2006).

4. Midas Dekkers, *The Way of All Flesh: The Romance of Ruins* (New York: Farrar, Straus & Giroux, 2000), 50.

5. John 1:46.

6. The facts concerning William Webb Ellis and the origins of rugby are apocryphal. This is one version of many. For additional information, see "Historical Rugby," http://wesclark.com/rrr/history.html (accessed 6 October 2006).

7. Leonard Sweet, "Trash Cans or Treasure Chests," a sermon preached at Ginghamsburg United Methodist Church, 28–29 August 1999, www.ginghamsburg.org/sermon99/aug2999.htm (accessed 13 April 2006). The original source for this story cannot be found. If you are aware of the original source, please let me know at lenisweet@aol.com.

8. John 14:6.

9. John 8:32.

Chapter 3

1. Quoted in Walter Raymond Spaulding, "Why Music Is the Most Popular of the Fine Arts," *Etude* 57 (February 1939): 81, http:// repertoireonline.com/MusicCatalog/PUB/Etude%20030103.pdf (accessed 24 August 2006).

2. As of 16 May 2006 in Boulder, Colorado, Starbucks coffee cost $1.40 per twelve-ounce cup, so each ounce costs $0.1166666. A gallon equals one hundred twenty-eight ounces, so a gallon of Starbucks would cost $14.9333248 plus tax. (In Boulder, the total with tax would be $16.234424 per gallon.)

3. Bruce Horovitz, "Starbucks Aims Beyond Lattes to Extend Brand," *USA Today,* 19 May 2006, A2, http://usatoday.com/money/

industries/food/2006-05-18-starbucks-usat_x.htm (accessed 6 October 2006).

4. Marcia Mogelonsky, "A Hot Cup of…Yogurt?" *American Demographics,* November 1994, 4. In a little more than ten years (in 1993), this figure went from 1 percent to 20 to 30 percent of the coffee industry nationwide.

5. *National Coffee Drinking Trends* (New York: National Coffee Association of the U.S.A., 2005), 35. Of the USAmericans who drink coffee, 35 percent now use gourmet coffees, and the average age of these drinkers is 43.6.

6. Liza Picard, *Victorian London: The Life of a City, 1840–1870* (New York: St. Martin's, 2005), 81–82. One couple whose weekly earnings were 19s (shillings) 5d (pence), spent 5s a week on rent, and 8s 8d a week on bread, vegetables, meat/fish, milk, and beer. They spent another 2s 6d a week on coffee, tea, and sugar (the same amount as spent on meat/fish).

7. To calculate how expensive specialty coffee can be, check out www.hughchou.org/calc/coffee.cgi (accessed 8 September 2006).

8. See Revelation 3:16.

9. Joel Levy, *Really Useful: The Origins of Everyday Things* (Buffalo, NY: Firefly, 2002), 32. Nescafé, introduced in 1938, is still the world's leading brand of instant coffee.

10. I appreciate Winnipeg's Greg Glatz and his Starbucks-loving sister-in-law for helping me refine these thoughts.

11. Ann Saunders (senior vice-president for Starbucks marketing), quoted in David Kiley, "Best Global Brands: Protect Your Culture," *Business-Week,* 7 August 2006, 56, www.businessweek.com/magazine/content/06_32/b3996410.htm?chan=topStories_ssi_5 (accessed 10 August 2006).

12. B. Joseph Pine II and James H. Gilmore, *The Experience Economy: Work Is Theatre and Every Business a Stage* (Boston: Harvard Business School Press, 1999), 31. This is the thesis of Joseph Pine and James Gilmore,

who argue that the shift from rational to experiential, or as they put it, from absorption to immersion, is redrawing the global landscape.

13. *The Onion: America's Finest News Service,* 27 June 1998, www.theonion .com/content/node/29030 (accessed 14 September 2006).

14. While this anecdotal quote is a plausible statement, there is no known written source for it.

15. Brad Stone, "Grande Plans," *Newsweek,* 4 October 2004, 40–41, www.msnbc.msn.com/id/6100243/site/newsweek (accessed 13 July 2006).

16. Stone, "Grande Plans," 40. See the comments of John Glass, CIBC World Markets analyst.

17. Sheryl Gay Stolberg, "The Elusive Middle Ground," in "Week in Review," *The New York Times,* 29 May 2005, sec. 4, 1.

18. Daniel H. Pink, "The Shape of Things to Come," *Wired,* May 2003, 27, 30.

19. Hillel Schwartz, *Century's End: A Cultural History of the Fin de Siècle, from the 990s to the 1990s* (New York: Doubleday, 1990), 210. Hillel Schwartz, in his study of centuries' end, invents this word *janiformity* (named after the Roman god with faces looking in opposite directions) to express the nature of a world that sees multiples, the pervasive experiencing of life as both-and/and-also as reflected in phenomenon as different as guilt-free sin-food to cloning.

20. As far as I can tell, the phrase "the well curve" is that of Pink, "The Shape of Things to Come," 27, 30. In an e-mail from Pink on 26 June 2006, he confirmed my attribution.

21. "The Census Bureau reported in 2005 that 37 million people in the U.S. lived in poverty in 2004. That's 5.4 million more than in 2000—a 17 percent increase in a period when the number of people who weren't living in poverty edged up 2.5 percent." Peter Francese, "U.S. Consumer— Like No Other on the Planet," *Advertising Age,* 2 January 2006, 3.

22. Ferdinand Mount introduced the language of "uppers and downers" for talking about this in his book *Mind the Gap: Class in Britain Now* (London: Short Books, 2004), 75–114.

23. Laura D'Andrea Tyson (dean of London Business School), "How Bush Widened the Wealth Gap," *BusinessWeek*, 1 November 2004, 32. Mobility between social groups has declined over the past thirty years: the distribution of income and wealth in USAmerica has become more and more unequal. Among the world's major economies, the disparity in incomes between America's richest and everyone else is exceeded only by the wealth gaps in Mexico and Russia.

24. "The Town of the Talk," *The Economist*, 19 February 2005, 3.

25. Pinsent Masons, "Singapore Aims to Become a Cashless Society," *Out-Law News* (an e-commerce service of Pinsent Masons, a law firm based in London), 20 December 2000, www.out-law.com/page-1262 (accessed 26 July 2006).

26. "Dueling extremes" is Faith Popcorn's phrase, quoted in Bruce Horovitz, "Marketers Cater to Cravings and Remorse," *USA Today*, 8 May 2006, B1, www.usatoday.com/money/advertising/2006-05-08-dueling-extremes-usat2_x.htm (accessed 14 July 2006).

27. Horovitz, "Cravings and Remorse," B1.

28. See www.hersheys.com/products/chocolate.asp (accessed 5 October 2006) and click on Hershey's Sticks. Both companies allegedly came up with the same name independently. And I'm a Mars Bar.

Chapter 4

1. Mark Twain to Rev. J. H. Twitchel, 19 January 1897, in *Mark Twain's Letters*, ed. Albert Bigelow Paine (New York: Harper, 1929), 2:641.

2. Stefano Marzano, "Branding = Distinctive Authenticity," *Brand.New*, ed. Jane Pavitt (Princeton, NJ: Princeton University Press, 2000), 58.

3. "I don't have it in me to imitate the Son of God. I can't even imitate the sons and daughters of greatness. I'm not even going to try to be a Monet or a Mozart or a Georgia O'Keefe 'wannabee.' But what if Monet could paint his picture through me? What if O'Keefe could use my life as her brush? What if Jesus were to live his life through me? What if my life could become an instrument in God's hands?" Leonard Sweet, *Jesus Drives Me Crazy* (Grand Rapids: Zondervan, 2003), 53.

4. Vivian Bournazian, "Music History: Charlie Parker Took Jazz in a New Direction," *Voice of America*, 2 July 2005, www.voanews.com/specialenglish/archive/2005-07/2005-07-02-voa1.cfm (accessed 10 August 2006).

5. For more on this, see Esther de Waal, *Seeking God: The Way of St. Benedict* (Collegeville, MN: Liturgical Press, 1984), 121.

6. Alison Elliot, *The Miraculous Everyday* (Edinburgh, Scotland: Covenanters, 2005), 123, tells this story.

7. This distinction between "experiential" and "expressional" I draw from theologian Jürgen Moltmann, *The Spirit of Life: A Universal Affirmation* (Minneapolis: Fortress, 1992).

8. T. S. Eliot, "The Love Song of J. Alfred Prufrock," *The Complete Poems and Plays of T. S. Eliot* (London: Faber and Faber, 1969), 14.

9. Yann Martel, *Life of Pi: A Novel* (New York: Harcourt, 2001), 5.

10. David J. Lose, *Confessing Jesus Christ: Preaching in a Postmodern World* (Grand Rapids: Eerdmans, 2003), 233. Lose argues that this is where postmodernity pushes us.

11. Dorothee Soelle, *The Strength of the Weak: Toward a Christian Feminist Identity*, trans. Robert and Rita Kimber (Philadelphia: Westminster, 1984), 86. In Latin, this is *cogito Dei experimentalis,* or in English, "the perception of God through experience."

12. Paul used these words: "God was pleased through the foolishness of what was preached to save those who believe. Jews demand signs and Greeks look for wisdom, but we preach Christ crucified: a stumbling block to Jews and foolishness to Gentiles" (1 Corinthians 1:21–23, TNIV).

13. The Rationalist Posture was named in an essay by W. K. Clifford, "The Ethics of Belief," in his *The Ethics of Belief and Other Essays* (Amherst, NY: Prometheus, 1999), 77. For the Web version, see *The Ethics of Belief: Essays by William Kingdon Clifford, William James, A. J. Burger,* ed. A. J. Burger, 1997, 2001, http://ajburger.homstead.com/files/book .htm#ethics (accessed 29 January 2005).

14. Hebrews 11:1, KJV.

15. Pope John Paul II, "Fides et Ratio," *The Encyclicals of John Paul II,* ed. J. Michael Miller (Huntington, IN: Our Sunday Visitor, 2001), 871:38.1.

16. Proverbs 23:7, NKJV.

17. For more on this, see Raymond Tallis, "The Truth about Lies," *TLS: The Times Literary Supplement,* 21 December 2001, 3–4. While we think for ourselves, we must simultaneously submit our reasoning to the critique of others, since all of us have intellectual blind spots. Sir Arthur Conan Doyle, champion of rationality and deductive logic in his Sherlock Holmes character, was absolutely convinced of the existence of fairies. Historian Hugh Trevor-Roper, Oxford fellow and Cambridge Master, personally authenticated the obviously forged Hitler Diaries.

18. While we trust our intuitions, we must check our "interior knowledge" (Ignatius of Loyola) or our "inner knowings" (Mabel Boggs Sweet) with social urgings, since our own sense memories are less to be trusted at times than our communal memories. We all maintain fictions to help us keep writing the story of our lives, and every autobiography ever written stands corrected by the subsequent biographies. This was a

theme of Eric Hobsbawm in his Creighton Lecture, 8 November 1993, when he reminded us that the memory of participants is frequently at variance with the documentary record of what they did. Hobsbawm, *The Present as History: Writing the History of One's Own Times* (London: University of London, 1993).

19. See 2 John 1:4.

20. Isaiah 53:2, KJV.

21. Quoted in Nick Reding, "Java Man," *Fast Company,* May 2006, 73, www.fastcompany.com/magazine/105/food-coffee.html (accessed 20 June 2006). The New York Board of Trade (NYBOT) in Lower Manhattan certifies coffee "graders" or "cuppers."

22. Scott Bedbury, marketing director, quoted in Nicole Nolan, "Starbucked," *In These Times,* 11 November 1996, 14, quoted in Naomi Klein, *No Space, No Choice, No Jobs, No Logo: Taking Aim at the Brand Bullies* (New York: Picador, 2000), 138.

23. J. Stevenson, *The Catacombs: Rediscovered Monuments of Early Christianity* (London: Thames and Hudson, 1978), 20–23. There is even some evidence to suggest that they were regarded as a special caste of clergy. After AD 430, the fossores disappear from the record.

24. The phrase is that of Ambra Medda, "cofounder and director, Design Miami Basel, on a $10,400 Amanda Levete sofa," as quoted in Linda Tischler, "The Future of Design," *Fast Company,* July/August 2006, 59.

25. See Virginia Postrel, *The Substance of Style: How the Rise of Aesthetic Value Is Remaking Commerce, Culture, and Consciousness* (New York: HarperCollins, 2003), 56–57.

26. "Pots of Promise," *The Economist,* 24 May 2003, 70–71, www.economist.com/printedition/displayStory.cfm?Story_ID=1795852 (accessed 20 January 2005). This was a special report on the beauty business.

27. For an excellent rant against "designer spirituality," see Alan Hirsch, *The Forgotten Ways* (Grand Rapids: Brazos, 2006).

28. This ad resulted in an immediate increase in sales amounting to 3.4 percent. This is a huge increase in the soap market, where stable is success.

29. For more on this, see Belden C. Lane, "Biodiversity and the Holy Trinity," *America* 195 (17 December 2001): 10.

30. For more on this, see Pamela N. Danziger, *Why People Buy Things They Don't Need* (Chicago: Dearborn Trade Pub., 2004), 258–60.

31. See Revelation 3:16.

32. Petrarch is most known for this oxymoronic metaphor for sexual intensity. See Leonard Forster, *The Icy Fire: Five Studies in European Petrarchism* (New York: Cambridge University Press, 1969), 16–17.

33. Melvyn Bragg, *The Adventure of English* (New York: Arcade, 2003), 134.

34. See John 3:5. (I'm equating spirit with the fire of Pentecost here.)

35. This was really the essence of Karl Marx's critique of Christianity, as practiced in his day. Marx was right about some things.

36. This is an adaptation of a story I found in Hugh Martin, *The Parables of the Gospels and Their Meaning for Today* (New York: Abingdon Press, 1937), 96.

Chapter 5

1. As quoted by Frank Cottrell Boyce, "Ultimate Sessions," *The Tablet*, 20 May 2006, 25.

2. Jones Soda Co. is not unhappy that its main demographic is twelve- to twenty-four-year-olds, since they buy the bulk of sodas (spending over three hundred billion dollars annually) and are the future of the market, www.jonessoda.com/stockstuff/pdf_documents/jones_brochure.pdf (accessed 20 July 2000).

3. Check out www.photostamps.com (accessed 17 August 2006).

4. Manfred F. R. Kets de Vries, *The Leadership Mystique: A Users Manual for Human Enterprise* (London: Financial Times Prentice Hall, 2001), 60.

5. "The Rise of the Creative Consumer," *The Economist,* 12 March 2005, 59–60, www.economist.com/business/displayStory.cfm?story_id= 3749354 (accessed 20 July 2006).

6. Sara Rimensnyder, "Soundbite: Joystick Engineers," *Reason Online,* August/September 2003, www.reason.com/0308/soundbite.shtml (accessed 20 July 2006). University of Wisconsin Professor James Paul Gee says that games such as *Doom* actually improve visual attention skills by 30 percent, according to a study published in 2003. Gee's book *What Video Games Have to Teach Us About Learning and Literacy* argues that video games teach a "new literacy." The "writing" it teaches uses more than words—it uses pictures, video, and complex environments. For more on this, see James Paul Gee, *What Video Games Have to Teach Us About Learning and Literacy* (New York: Palgrave Macmillan, 2003), 13.

7. Quoted in Pamela Paul, "Nouveau Niche," *American Demographics,* July/August 2003, 21.

8. Jacques Steinberg, "For Gore, A Reincarnation on the Other Side of the Camera," *The New York Times,* 25 July 2005, C1.

9. Converse Gallery, www.conversegallery.com (accessed 20 July 2006). See also Laura Petrecca, "Amateur Advertisers Get a Chance," *USA Today,* 28 March 2006, B2, www.usatoday.com/money/advertising/ 2006-03-27-amateur-advertisers_x.htm (accessed 15 July 2006).

10. Leander Kahney, *The Cult of iPod* (San Francisco: No Starch Press, 2005). For more on this, also see "Circuit City Dumps VHS for DVD," *MediaLine,* 4 February 2005, www.medialinenews.com/issues/2002/ june/news0620_2.shtml (accessed 4 February 2005). Almost as soon as Circuit City began phasing out VHS movies in 2002, with some of its more than six hundred stores immediately halting sales, the iPod made its appearance and wiped out DVDs.

11. Matthew Mirapaul, "Why Just Listen to Pop When You Can Mix Your Own," *The New York Times,* late edition (East Coast), 20 August 2001, E2.

12. David Rocks and Chen Wu, "A Phoenix Named Flying Pigeon," *BusinessWeek,* 20 September 2004, www.businessweek.com/magazine/content/04_38/b3900077.htm (accessed 8 February 2005).

13. I am foregoing for the moment the whole arena of religion, which is being reshaped by "P" (participation). For the participatory development of religious beliefs, see Carl L. Bankston III, "Rationality, Choice and the Religious Economy: The Problem of Belief," *Review of Religious Research* 43 (2002): 311–25.

14. A couple of examples: (1) the Hollywood fund-raiser for victims of 9/11 encouraged you to call in and talk to the stars, and (2) basically all the NBC shows now auction off "walk-on" roles for charity auctions: you can bid to spend the day on a set and be a part of a scene.

15. Almost thirty-five million viewers watched *American Idol,* while only twenty-some million watched the Grammys.

16. The Fox talent show walloped the 2006 Olympics by eleven million more USAmerican viewers.

17. For more on this, see the cover story by Elysa Gardner and Bill Keveney, "Fox Hit 'American Idol' Mixes Music, Meanness: Skeptics Wonder if This Is the Way to Pick Stars," *USA Today,* 30 July 2002, A1–2.

18. Anjanette Flowers, "Clay Aiken Accepts Education Degree," *News 14 Carolina,* 20 December 2006, www.news14charlotte.com/content/local_news/?ArID=49364&SecID=2 (accessed 15 July 2006).

19. For more on this, see William L. Benzon, *Beethoven's Anvil: Music in Mind and Culture* (New York: Basic, 2001), 280.

20. One segment of the voting-age demographic already has tipped the scale in favor of reality TV. "More people between the ages of 18 and

24 voted for *American Idol* than voted in the [2000] election." Mark J. Miller, interview by MTV news correspondent Gideon Yago, "Watching Iraq: Is the Reporting about Iraq Info You Can Use or a Big Snooze," *Teen People,* 1 June 2003, 114.

21. I realize I am arguing here with Marshall McLuhan, who defined television as a "cool" medium, that is, one in which consumers felt they were participants, as opposed to a "hot" medium such as radio where, McLuhan argued, listeners were more like passive recipients (for example, few people talk back to a radio; many do to a television set). But if TV is a cool medium, then the Internet is a frozen medium.

22. For more on this, see Monica Brasted, "Through the Looking Glass: Class and Reality in Television," *Electronic Journal of Sociology,* 2004, www.sociology.org/content/2004/tier2/brasted.html (accessed 4 August 2006). SUNY Professor Dr. Monica Brasted found in her research that the Internet tends to subvert the status quo, while television supports the prevailing social, political, and moral norms.

23. Marshall Sella, "The Remote Controllers," *The New York Times Magazine,* 20 October 2002, 68. Most reality shows around the world now encourage text-message voting. But more than voting, all TV shows are now becoming two-way streets. *The X-Files* started the "boards" (message boards) in the 1990s, with Fox and WB first picking up text messaging as an integral part of the television experience.

24. Tom Lowry and Ronald Grover, "Football's Fear Factor: Why the TV Networks Are Throwing Cash at the NFL," *BusinessWeek,* 22 November 2004, 157. CBS and Fox will spend eight billion dollars through 2011 for the rights to broadcast NFL games on Sunday afternoons. Each pro sports league gets licensing revenue from video games, some of which are in the hundreds of millions of dollars. In 2004 the NFL got three hundred million dollars from a five-year licensing deal with Electronic Arts (a leading video game company).

25. Lowry and Grover, "Football's Fear Factor," 157. As of 2005 the NFL's
    ratings are down almost 9 percent since 1998, but its broadcasts still
    average 15.5 million viewers, according to Nielsen Media Research.
26. Seth Schiesel, "They Got (Video) Game: N.B.A. Finals Can Wait,"
    The New York Times, 21 June 2005, late edition (East Coast), A1, A18.
    "Since 2000, television broadcast ratings for almost all major sports
    have fallen among male viewers between 12 and 34. Even NASCAR,
    whose ratings have generally been hailed by the industry as healthy, has
    suffered a modest decline, according to Nielsen Media Research. Over
    the same period, sales of sports video games in the US have risen by
    about 34 percent, to more than $1.2 billion last year from slightly less
    than $900 million in 2000, according to the NPD Group."
27. National Sporting Goods Association, www.nsga.org (accessed 4 August
    2006).
28. "On the newsstands publications about fantasy outnumbered the tradi-
    tional previews about the upcoming season." Tim Wendel, "How Fan-
    tasy Games Have Changed Fans," *USA Today,* 20 September 2004, A23,
    www.usatoday.com/news/opinion/editorials/20040919oplede_x.htm
    (accessed 5 February 2005). Wendel also notes that fantasy sports is
    now a 1.65 billion dollar industry, with twenty million–plus participants
    in USAmerica alone. The key to fantasy sports is that you don't focus
    on or follow real teams, you follow players. Each person is an owner,
    and owners select pro stars for their make-believe teams where statistical
    feats determine success.
29. Schiesel, "They Got (Video) Game," A18.
30. California's tendency toward direct citizen rule through recall and refer-
    endum, which bypasses gridlocked legislatures, is a foretaste of the
    future.
31. "Reshaping Political Values in the Information Age—The Power of the
    Media," address by Lawrence K. Grossman, former president of PBS

and NBC News, delivered to the Everett C. Parker Ethics in Telecommunications Lecture, New York, New York, 17 September 1996, *Vital Speeches of the Day* 63 (15 January 1997), 209.

32. Edwin Schlossberg, *Interactive Excellence: Defining and Developing New Standards for the Twenty-first Century* (New York: Ballantine, 1998).

33. Schlossberg, *Interactive Excellence,* 98.

34. For more on this, see Thomas de Zengotita, *Mediated: How the Media Shapes Your World and the Way You Live in It* (New York: Bloomsbury, 2005), 115.

35. This became almost a signature ritual of the redemption song "Alive."

Chapter 6

1. Luke 1:38; see John 1:1–15; see Colossians 2:9.

2. This is from "Mary's Song," found in Luke 1:46–55. The quote is from verse 53.

3. Frank Gehry has said, "I'll only work with clients who are willing to work closely with me, to be a part of the process from the beginning until the end," in Gehry, "The AD 100: The International Directory of Interior Designers and Architects," *Architectural Digest,* January 2004, 61, www.architecturaldigest.com/design/AD100/articles/040713de_027 (accessed 7 February 2005).

4. For more on the way in which modernity reduced thought to a system and a formula, making "rational" representational, whereas in premodern culture it was participational, see the work of theologian David Tracy, "Public Theology, Hope, and the Mass Media: Can the Muses Still Inspire?" *Religion and the Powers of the Common Life,* vol. 1 of *God and Globalization,* ed. Max L. Stackhouse with Peter J. Paris (Harrisburg, PA: Trinity Press International, 2000), 246–47.

5. When they learn how to screen out unwanted content, they promise to be back.

6. Marty Hagen, interview by Ellen Teague, "Minister of Sound," *The Tablet*, 26 November 2005, 14.

7. John Drury, "Poetry and Truth," *Public Life and the Place of the Church: Reflections to Honour the Bishop of Oxford*, ed. Michael Brierley (Burlington, VT: Ashgate, 2006), 154.

8. 2 Timothy 1:7, NRSV.

9. John Bunyan, "Of Justification by an Imputed Righteousness. Or, No Way to Heaven but by Jesus Christ," *The Miscellaneous Works of John Bunyan*, ed. Roger Sharrock (Oxford: Clarendon, 1994), 12:341.

10. Ralph L. Lewis with Gregg Lewis, *Learning to Preach Like Jesus* (Westchester, Ill.: Crossway Books, 1989), 22.

11. "Like a Rolling Stone," by Bob Dylan, was rated number one in "500 Greatest Songs of All Time," *Rolling Stone*, Special Collectors Issue, 9 December 2004, www.rollingstone.com/news/story/6595846/like_a_rolling_stone (accessed 30 July 2006).

12. Al Kooper, *Backstage Passes and Backstabbing Bastards: Memories of a Rock 'n Roll Survivor* (New York: Billboard Books, 1998), 34–38. This story is now available on video, told by Kooper himself, in Martin Scorsese's movie *No Direction Home: Bob Dylan* (2005).

13. I believe Jesus chose to limit his foreknowledge as part of his fully-man-of-fully-man status. In living life to its fullest (see John 10:10), he chose to enjoy the spontaneity of human existence that adds energy and pleasure to life.

14. See Luke 19:5.

15. Dominican friar Timothy Radcliffe makes the crucial distinction between superficial spontaneity and deep spontaneity: "So spontaneity is not doing the first thing that comes into one's head. It is acting from the core of one's being, where God is, sustaining one in existence." In fact, deep spontaneity may be a kind of "freedom of choice" where there are fewer choices, not more; where freedom means being free to

do what *must* be done. "At the Last Supper Jesus performs the freest act in human history. He gives away his life: 'this is my body, given for you.' It appears an almost reckless act, placing himself in the hands of his disciples, the very people who will betray and deny him, and run away from him. It even looks like the loss of all freedom." Timothy Radcliffe, "Learning Spontaneity," *What Is the Point of Being a Christian?* (New York: Burns & Oats, 2005), 43, 46.

16. *House of Sand and Fog,* DVD, produced by Michael London and Vadim Perelman (Universal City, CA: DreamWorks Home Entertainment, 2003), based on Andre Dubus III, *House of Sand and Fog* (New York: Norton, 1999).

17. Patricia Treece, *A Man for Others: Maximilian Kolbe, Saint of Auschwitz, in the Words of Those Who Knew Him* (San Francisco: Harper & Row), 1982), 170–76.

18. Eamon Duffy, *Walking to Emmaus* (New York: Burns & Oates, 2006), 24.

19. For more on this, see Leonard Sweet, "The Nerve of Failure," *Theology Today,* July 1977, 142–49.

20. This is the crux of the problem of Islam in postmodern culture: it is structurally not set up as a religion to tolerate contradictory ideas. It is too easy to say that Al Qaeda is to Islam what KKK is to Christianity. What is going on is more complex and worrisome than that. Intrinsic to Christianity is the celebration of difference; intrinsic to Judaism is debate and discourse over interpretations of the Talmud; intrinsic to Islam is the inability to abide difference.

21. See Matthew 13:13–15.

22. Jacques Derrida, *The Gift of Death,* trans. David Wills (Chicago: University of Chicago Press, 1995).

23. For more on this, see the Web site of Dwight Friesen, www.dwight friesen.com (accessed 12 August 2006).

24. For a poetic exploration of this theme, see "We only live, only conspire / Consumed by either fire or fire," in T. S. Eliot, "Little Gidding," *Four Quartets,* stanza 4, last two lines.

25. Christ is sprezzaturish. He is an endless combination of many things at once: divine and human, crucified and resurrected, earthly and eternal, abased and victorious, wounded and whole.

26. Adin Steinsaltz, *Simple Words: Thinking About What Really Matters in Life* (New York: Touchstone, 2001), 61.

27. Martin Luther King Jr., *Letter from the Birmingham Jail, 1963* (San Francisco: HarperSanFrancisco, 1994), 23.

28. "The truth is precisely the venture which chooses an objective uncertainty with the passion of the infinite." *Kierkegaard's Concluding Unscientific Postscript,* trans. David F. Swenson and Walter Lowrie (Princeton, NJ: Princeton University Press, 1944), 182.

29. For more of these, see "From Sharp to Fuzzy," in my *Carpe Mañana: Is Your Church Ready to Seize Tomorrow?* (Grand Rapids: Zondervan, 2000), 125–36.

30. *"Et animasti me, domine, qui es cibus grandium, ut vim mihi ipse faciam, quia impossibilitas coincidet cum necessitate. Et repperi locum in quo revelate reperieris, cinctum contradictoriorum coincidentia. Et iste est murus paradisi in quo habitas, cuius portam custodit spiritus altissimus rationis, qui nisi vincatur, no patebit ingressus."* "And I have found the abode wherein You dwell unveiledly—an abode surrounded by the coincidence of contradictories. And [this coincidence] is the wall of Paradise, wherein You dwell. The gate of this wall is guarded by a most lofty rational spirit; unless this spirit is vanquished the entrance will not be accessible." Jasper Hopkins, trans. and ed., *Nicholas of Cusa's Dialectical Mysticism, Text, Translation, and Interpretive Study of De Visione Dei,* 2nd ed. (Minneapolis: Arthur J. Banning, 1988), 160 (Latin), 161 (English).

31. Wallace Stevens, "Esthetique du Mal," *Transport to Summer* (New York: Knopf, 1947), 46.

Chapter 7

1. Quoted in Dana Toomey, "Imaging Peace: The Soul/Body Connection," *Spirituality & Health,* Summer 2000, 43.

2. Quoted in David Martin, "Holy Matrimony I," *Christian Language in the Secular City* (Burlington, VT: Ashgate, 2002), 200.

3. As explained by a youngster on CBS's *48 Hours* (3 February 2002) and later published in John Killinger, *God, The Devil, and Harry Potter: A Christian Minister's Defense of the Beloved Novels* (New York: Thomas Dunne, 2002), 7.

4. Quoted in Toomey, "Imaging Peace," 43.

5. Philip Pullman calls Christianity "a very powerful and convincing mistake" (128), and he despises C. S. Lewis, especially The Chronicles of Narnia. For more on this, see Michael Ward, "Philip Pullman's Attack on Narnia: A Defense," *Mars Hill Review* 21, 2003, 127–35.

6. Philip Pullman was also named Author of the Year at the British Book Awards.

7. Philip Pullman, "Carnegie Medal Acceptance Speech," www.random house.com/features/pullman/philippullman/speech.html (accessed 31 January 2005).

8. For a description and a look at Thalassa, see pages 99 and 278 (fig. 14) in Peter Dronke, *Imagination in the Late Pagan and Early Christian World: The First Nine Centuries A.D.* (Florence, Italy: Sismel, 2003). To see Thalassa on the Internet, go to www.vazyvite.com/photo_div/ jordanie/madaba_thalassa.jpg (accessed 5 October 2006).

9. H. B. Wheatley, introduction to *Stow's Survey of London,* by John Stow (New York: Dutton, 1956), 361. Originally published as John Stow, *A Survey of London: Containing the Originall, Antiquity, Increase,*

Moderne Estate, and Description of that City (1598; repr., London: Iohn Windet, 1603).

10. The original Starbucks mermaid logo had protruding breasts and a split fish tail. This was deemed too overtly sexual, so it was toned down to its current form. The only place you can find the original logo of the mermaid is at Mother Starbucks in Seattle.

11. Lauren Young, "The Spa, 'Starbucked,'" *BusinessWeek*, 31 July 2006, 77.

12. Howard Schultz and Don Jones Yang, *Pour Your Heart Into It: How Starbucks Built a Company One Cup at a Time* (New York: Hyperion, 1997), 243–46.

13. Joseph Michelli, *The Starbucks Experience: 5 Principles for Turning Ordinary into Extraordinary* (New York: McGraw-Hill, 2006), says it is 250 percent lower than the industry average.

14. Paul Ginsborg, *The Politics of Everyday Life: Making Choices, Changing Lives* (New Haven: Yale University Press, 2005), 86.

15. For the movement of students around the country who have successfully persuaded food-service administrators to serve only coffee that comes with a Fair Trade label, see United Students for Fair Trade, www.usft.org (accessed 14 August 2006).

16. "The Fair Trade mark is only granted to products where certain conditions are met, the most important being that small-scale farmers can participate in democratic organisations of their own, that plantation or factory workers have the right to join trade unions and are assured of decent wages as well as decent working conditions and housing, that there is no child labour or forced labour, and that there is a clear strategy for environmental sustainability." Ginsborg, *Politics of Everyday Life*, 84–85.

Chapter 8

1. See, for example, Deuteronomy 14:2 and 26:18, KJV.

2. Revelation 21:1.

3. Tore Frängsmyr and Sture Allen, eds., *Nobel Lectures, Including Presentation Speeches and Laureates' Biographies: Literature, 1969–1980* (Singapore: World Scientific, 1993), 46. Also Aleksandr Solzhenitsyn lecture, "The Nobel Prize in Literature 1970," http://nobelprize.org/nobel_prizes/literature/laureates/1970/solzhenitsyn-lecture.html (accessed 2 August 2006).

4. Genesis 2:5, KJV.

5. What came first: the image or the reality? Slovenian philosopher Slavoj Zizek noted four days after 9/11 how America imagined a 9/11 attack in films such as *Independence Day* and *Escape from New York*. See Slavoj Zizek, "Welcome to the Desert of the Real," *Re:Constructions: Reflections on Humanity and Media After Tragedy,* 15 September 2001, http://web.mit.edu/cms/reconstructions/interpretations/desertreal.html (accessed 31 July 2006).

6. For the preacher as "custodian of metaphor," see James A. Wallace, *Imaginal Preaching: An Archetypal Perspective* (New York: Paulist Press, 1995), 19. The phrase "stewards of the mysteries" comes from 1 Co-rinthians 4:1, KJV. For more on Jesus as the Metanarrative, see my *Three Hardest Words in the World to Get Right* (Colorado Springs: WaterBrook, 2006).

7. Rob Weber, *Visual Leadership: The Church Leaders as ImageSmith* (Nashville: Abingdon, 2003).

8. John Donne, "The Second of My Prebend Sermons upon My Five Psalmes, Preached at S. Pauls, Ianuary 29, 1625," *Donne's Prebend Sermons,* ed. Janel M. Mueller (Cambridge: Harvard University Press, 1971), 105 (lines 410–11).

9. Matthew 26:73, NASB.

10. Other words that might work just as well are *talisman, token,* and *keepsake.*

11. Gerard W. Hughes, *God in All Things* (London: Hodder & Stoughton, 2003), 75.

12. 1 Corinthians 15:46, TNIV.

13. Notice how, when reality TV shows like *American Idol* and *The Apprentice* enter their final weeks, the news media cover them as real news events.

14. David Crouch, *Tournament* (London: Hambledon and London, 2005), 1, 111, 116. Twelfth-century Templar Knight William Marshal I, Earl of Pembroke, "the best and most loyal knight in his world" (16), did achieve political significance in a way seemingly forbidden to modern sporting celebrities.

15. Lucas Conley, "Summer Reading with a Twist," *Fast Company*, July/August 2006, 101–3, www.fastcompany.com/magazine/107/playbook-summer-reading.html (accessed 31 July 2006).

16. And then there is the megachurch phenomenon, which is taking celebrity culture in new directions not yet fully understood. Shane Hipps talks about video venues enabling us to "say goodbye to the priesthood of all believers and hello to the papacy of celebrity." Shane Hipps, *Hidden Power of Electronic Culture: How Media Shapes Faith, the Gospel, and Church* (Grand Rapids: Zondervan, 2006), 152.

17. I can date my rude awakening to the power of celebrity culture. It came after I told a story to a group of Salvation Army officers and their spouses. I was comparing how the United Methodist Church, my "tribe," in 2000 allocated twenty-four million dollars to launch a media campaign (Open Hearts, Open Minds, Open Doors), the same year another media campaign was launched for the same amount of money. The second campaign was promoting a motion picture that focused not on getting more people to attend a particular denomination, but to tell the story of Jesus. Not the whole story. Just a couple of hours in that story. And to tell it with as much authenticity as possible—which meant an R rating for the violence of crucifixion and the script delivered in the original languages.

The Passion of the Christ turned out to be the largest-grossing R-rated movie in history. It has made more than $300 million. My tribe asked for another twenty-four million dollars in 2004 to keep the Open Hearts media campaign going, making a total investment of almost fifty million dollars that still has not stopped the hemorrhaging of the denomination's membership rolls. In contrast, Gibson's investment of twenty-four million dollars has made him the bankroller for promising film directors. When I first told this story, my basic point was that God was not going to be without a witness. And if my tribe was telling its own story rather than the story of Jesus, then God would raise up people like Mel Gibson to tell the gospel story in a way that the culture could hear it.

After I was done, the wife of a Salvation Army general asked if she could speak to me privately. "Dr. Sweet, I was at *The Oprah Show* the day that *The Passion of the Christ* was set to be released. We were standing in the corridors, waiting for the doors to open so we could get good seats in the studio audience, when suddenly someone came and announced to all of us that today's show would be a live broadcast, not a taped segment. Oprah had arranged for a special guest to come and debut their newest project.

"When they left, Dr. Sweet, I'll never forget how giddy we all got. Everyone there *knew* it had to be Mel Gibson, and we were so excited. I remember high-fiving other people there in the excitement of the moment. We were going to be on *The Oprah Show* with Mel Gibson. When the doors opened and we walked into the studio, it was like we were walking on air.

"Well, it turned out it wasn't Mel Gibson who was Oprah's guest that day."

I smiled, still not sure where she was going with her story. The next words out of her mouth, though, changed my whole thinking about celebrity culture.

"I'm not sure, Dr. Sweet, that any one of us in the corridor that day would have been nearly as excited as we were if we had thought that it was the United Methodist Church with Oprah that day for the world premier of a movie called *The Passion of the Christ*."

18. Thomas de Zengotita, *Mediated: How the Media Shapes Your World and the Way You Live in It* (New York: Bloomsbury, 2005), 115.

19. Psychologists at the University of Leicester have identified the CWS syndrome, an obsessive addictive behavior that affects one in three people to some degree and may become a "serious clinical issue." For more see John Maltby, James Houran, and Lynn E. McCutcheon, "A Clinical Interpretation of Attitudes and Behaviors Associated with Celebrity Worship," *Journal of Nervous and Mental Disease* 191 (January 2003): 25–29.

20. The best books on this are George Barna, *Revolution* (Wheaton, IL: Tyndale, 2005) and Bob Roberts, *Transformation: How Glocal Churches Transform Lives and the World* (Grand Rapids: Zondervan, 2006).

21. Abdel Bari Atwan, *The Secret History of al Qaida* (Berkeley: University of California Press, 2006), 120. Bin Laden's acolytes have studies at his feet. On 29 June 2005, the late Abu Musab al-Zarqawi released "All Religion Will Be for Allah," a forty-six minute video of live-action war, made directly for the Internet. You could choose Windows Media Player or RealPlayer to access it. Susan B. Glasser and Steve Coll, "The Web as Weapon," *The Washington Post*, 9 August 2005, A01, www .washingtonpost.com/wp-dyn/content/article/2005/08/08/AR2005 080801018.html (accessed 6 October 2006).

22. Charles Glass, "Cyber-Jihad," *London Review of Books*, 9 March 2006, 14. "While the US military lowers entrance requirements and raises pay, Osama's guarantee of hardship, hunger and probable death has young Muslims jumping the jihad queue.... If he endorses a war in, say Iraq,

the roads clog with volunteers," www.lrb.co.uk/v28/n05/glas01_.html (accessed 31 July 2006).

23. In many ways U2's Bono has replaced Mother Teresa in celebrity culture.

24. Quoted in de Zengotita, *Mediated,* 117.

25. W. J. T. Mitchell introduces a tripartite concept of the object as idol, fetish, and totem in *What Do Pictures Want? The Lives and Loves of Images* (Chicago: University of Chicago Press, 2005), 26.

26. This is a common phrase taken from Laura Gascoigne, "Through the Eyes of Faith," *The Tablet,* 29 April 2006, 32.

27. See Friedrich Nietzsche, *The Twilight of the Idols, or How to Philosophize with a Hammer,* trans. Duncan Large (New York: Oxford University Press, [1889] 1998), 3.

Chapter 9

1. Hester Lynch Piozzi, *Anecdotes of the Late Samuel Johnson, LLD, During the Last Twenty Years of His Life* (Dublin, Ireland: printed for Messrs. Moncrieffe, White, Byrne, Cash, W. Porter, Marchbank, M'Kenzie, Moore, and Jones, 1786), electronic resource, 266–67.

2. Bruce Sterling, *Tomorrow Now: Envisioning the Next Fifty Years* (New York: Random House, 2002), 235.

3. Blogging is an example of people wanting to control their media rather than being controlled by it.

4. Paul Ginsborg, *The Politics of Everyday Life: Making Choices, Changing Lives* (New Haven, CT: Yale University, 2005), 76.

5. Ray Oldenburg, *The Great Good Place: Cafés, Coffee Shops, Community Centers, Beauty Parlors, General Stores, Bars, Hangouts, and How They Get You Through the Day* (New York: Paragon, 1989), 22–42.

6. Quoted in Richard Pascale, "The False Security of 'Employability,'" *FastCompany,* April 1996, 62. This is an adaptation from Oldenburg, *The Great Good Place,* xv.

7. For more information on U2 and DATA, visit www.data.org (accessed 17 August 2006) and http://jam.canoe.ca/Music/Artists/U/U2 (accessed 6 October 2006).

8. Quoted in Taylor Engler, "Starbucks Offers Caffeinated Release from the Daily Grind," *The Daily Orange,* 18 January 2006, www.dailyorange .com/media/storage/paper522/news/2006/01/18/Pulp/Starbucks.Offers .Caffeinated.Release.From.The.Daily.Grind-1434460.shtml?norewrite 200609131559&sourcedomain=www.dailyorange.com (accessed 7 August 2006). *The Daily Orange* is the independent student newspaper of Syracuse University.

9. Michele Norris, "Porches Knit Together New Urbanists Communities," www.npr.org/templates/story/story.php?storyId=5597920 (accessed 7 August 2006).

10. Hassan Fattah, "America Untethered," *American Demographics,* March 2003, 35–39, www.upoc.com/corp/news/UpocAmDem.pdf (accessed 7 August 2006).

11. "The March of the Mobiles," *The Economist,* 25 September 2004, 16.

12. "The Starbucks Experience," company profile, August 2005, www.star bucks.com/aboutus/CompanyProfileFeb05.pdf (accessed 7 August 2006).

Chapter 10

1. Catherine of Siena, *Catherine of Siena: Passion for the Truth, Compassion for Humanity: Selected Spiritual Writings,* ed. Mary O'Driscoll (New York: New City, 1993), 97.

2. Matthew Creamer, "Do You Know Your Score?" *Advertising Age,* 3 July 2006, 1, 24.

3. Ben McConnell and Jackie Huba, "Learning to Leverage the Lunatic Fringe: The Six Tenets of Customer Evangelism," in "Point," *Advertising Age: Point,* July/August 2006, 14. McConnell and Huba are the authors of *Creating Customer Evangelists: How Loyal Customers Become*

a Volunteer Sales Force (Chicago: Dearborn Trade Publishing, 2003). They are also founders of the Church of the Customer blog: www .churchofthecustomer.com/blog (accessed 6 October 2006).

4. Fred Reichheld, *The Ultimate Question: Driving Good Profits and True Growth* (Boston: Harvard Business School Press, 2006), 18–19, 195. The actual question is: "How likely is it that you would recommend our company to a friend or colleague?" The NPS (Net Promoter Score) is figured by subtracting detractors—a.k.a. sinners—(those who gave a 0–6 on a 0–10 scale) from promoters—a.k.a. winners (those who gave a 9 or 10 on a 0–10 scale).

5. Liebmann is president of WSL Strategic Retail.

6. Zygmunt Bauman, *Liquid Love: On the Frailty of Human Bonds* (Cambridge, UK: Polity, 2003), 59.

7. E. M. Forster, *Howards End* (Garden City, NY: Garden City, 1921), title page.

8. John Drew, letter to the editor, "Proscribed Forster," *TLS: The Times Literary Supplement,* 27 December 2002, 13.

9. For more on this idea, see Esther de Waal, *Living with Contradiction: An Introduction to Benedictine Spirituality* (Harrisburg, PA: Morehouse, 1989), 13–15.

10. Paraphrase of Colossians 1:17, NRSV and TNIV: "In him all things hold together."

11. Genesis 15:1.

12. William Willimon, ed., "People Don't Change, Do They," *Pulpit Resource* (January, February, March 1994), 17. This quote was inspired by ideas contained in *The Screwtape Letters* that refer to God's love for the "little vermin" of humanity, while honoring their individuality and free will: "Remember, always, that He really likes the little vermin, and sets an absurd value on the distinctness of every one of them. When He talks of their losing their selves, He means only abandoning the clamour

of self-will; once they have done that, He really gives them back all their personality, and boasts (I am afraid, sincerely) that when they are wholly His, they will be more themselves than ever." C. S. Lewis, *The Screwtape Letters* (New York: Bantam, 1995), 38.

13. See John 15:15, TNIV.

14. John 15:15, TNIV.

15. C. Robert Jennings, interview, "Mae West: A Candid Conversation with the Indestructible Queen of Vamp and Camp," *Playboy*, January 1971, 82.

16. Chris Seay turned me on to John McKnight, who helped me see how Jesus consistently forefronts relational language that does not have the hierarchical components of the servant/lord language. "Why friends rather than servants? Perhaps it is because He knew that servants could always become lords but that friends could not. Servants are people who know the mysteries that can control those to whom they give 'help.' Friends are people who know each other. They are free to give and receive help." John McKnight, *The Careless Society: Community and Its Counterfeits* (New York: Basic, 1995), 179. Servant leadership is positional. Friend leadership is relational.

17. This is the thesis of Ellen Dissanayake: art is "making special" behavior that is "sensorily and emotionally gratifying and more than strictly necessary." See her *Homo Aestheticus: Where Art Comes From and Why* (New York: Free Press, 1992), 56.

18. See the remarkable story of this Brit who chained himself to a building in Rangoon denouncing the regime of tyranny. The quote is from James Mawdsley, *The Iron Road: A Stand for Truth and Democracy in Burma* (New York: North Point Press, 2002), 108. Originally published as *The Heart Must Break: Burma—Democracy and Truth* (London: Century, 2001), 116.

19. For more on the theme of being knit together, see Job 10:11; Psalm 139:13; 1 Chronicles 12:17, KJV; and Ephesians 4:16, NKJV.

20. Kathleen Kovner Kline, ed., *Hardwired to Connect: The New Scientific Case for Authoritative Communities: A Report to the Nation* (New York: Institute for American Values, 2003), 2. The three partners in the "Commission on Children at Risk" were the YMCA of the USA, Dartmouth Medical School, and the Institute for American Values.

21. Robert A. Boisture, ed., "Summary of the Commission on Children at Risk's Report: *Hardwired to Connect: The New Scientific Case for Authoritative Communities*" (Washington DC: YMCA of the USA, 2003), 4–5.

22. Boisture, "Summary of the Commission on Children at Risk's Report," 6. The definition of "authoritative communities" is as follows: "groups of people who are committed to one another over time and who model and pass on at least part of what it means to be a good person and live a good life. Essentially, they are groups that live out the types of connectedness that our children increasingly lack. The family is (or at least should be) the most important authoritative community. Other core authoritative communities include youth organizations such as YMCAs, other community groups involved with children, religious organizations, and schools."

23. Boisture, "Summary of the Commission on Children at Risk's Report," 17.

24. McKnight, *Careless Society,* xi.

25. Kline, *Hardwired to Connect,* 34. The ten main characteristics of an authoritative community ("a social institution that includes children and youth") might be summed up this way: a "nurturing" environment focused on the "principle of love of neighbor" with "clear limits and expectations" and "spiritual and religious development."

26. Nelson Mandela, *The Long Walk to Freedom: The Autobiography of Nelson Mandela* (Boston: Little Brown, 1994), 624.

27. Robert Putnam, *Bowling Alone: The Collapse and Revival of American Community* (New York: Simon & Schuster, 2000), 22. Putnam says he got this distinction from Ross Gittell and Avis Vidal, *Community Organizing: Building Social Capital as a Development Strategy* (Thousand Oaks, CA: Sage, 1998), 8; see also 24, 26, 178.

28. Mark 14:22, NKJV.

29. Mark 14:24.

30. Ephesians 4:25, KJV.

31. For further elaboration of this distinction between the two blessings, one inward toward koinonia and one outward toward kingdom, see Timothy Radcliffe, "Root Shock," in *What Is the Point of Being a Christian?* (New York: Burns & Oats, 2005), 164–78.

32. Ephesians 2:17, NRSV.

33. Check out Psalm 148.

Epilogue

1. Quoted in Gail Edmondson, "*Basta* with the Venti Frappuccinos: Illy-caffè Is the Anti-Starbucks—and It's Out to Spread the Espresso Gospel to Java Heathens," *BusinessWeek,* 7 August 2006, 42, www.business week.com/magazine/content/06_32/b3996057.htm?chan=search (accessed 6 October 2006).

2. Islamic Food and Nutrition Council of America, "Caffeine," *Halal Digest,* November 2000, 2, www.ifanca.org/newsletter/2000_11.pdf (accessed 13 July 2006).

3. See Song of Solomon 1:5, KJV.

4. See 1 Kings 10:1–2.

5. The common word for both "bean" and "prayer" is *bønne.* Steve Sjogren points this out in his introduction to *Seeing Beyond Church Walls:*

Action Plans for Touching Your Community (Loveland, CO: Group, 2002), 9.

6. See the excellent chapter on "Coffee and the Protestant Ethic" in Wolfgang Schivelbusch, *Tastes of Paradise: A Social History of Spices, Stimulants, and Intoxicants* (New York: Pantheon, 1994), 15–84.

7. Steven Shapin, "At the Amsterdam," *London Review of Books*, 20 April 2006, 12.

8. Tom Standage, *A History of the World in 6 Glasses* (New York: Walker, 2005), 136.

9. Schivelbusch, *Tastes of Paradise*, 38–39.

10. Adam Smyth, ed., *A Pleasing Sinne: Drink and Conviviality in Seventeenth-Century England* (Cambridge, UK: D. S. Brewer, 2004), xviii.

11. Stewart Lee Allen, *The Devil's Cup: The Driving Force in History* (New York: Soho, 1999), 129.

12. Allen, *Devil's Cup*, 129.

13. Allen, *Devil's Cup*, 134.

14. Quoted in Schivelbusch, *Tastes of Paradise*, 34–35.

15. "The Internet in a Cup," *The Economist*, 20 December 2003, 88–89, www.economist.com/World/europe/displayStory.cfm?story_id=2281736 (accessed 15 June 2005).

16. "The Internet in a Cup," 88.

17. Norma Clarke, "Before Latte," *TLS: Times Literary Supplement*, November 2004, 11, reviewing Markman Ellis, *The Coffee House: A Cultural History* (London: Weidenfeld and Nicolson, 2005), 68–71.

18. Ellis, *The Coffee House*, 89.

19. Standage, *History of the World*, 144.

20. Stephen Miller, *Conversation: A History of a Declining Art* (New Haven, CT: Yale University Press, 2006).

21. Isaac Bickerstaff [Richard Steele], "No. 21. From Thursday, May 26, to Saturday, May 28, 1709: White's Chocolate-House, May 26," ed.

George A. Aitken, *The Tatler* (New York: Hadley and Mathews, 1899), 1:175, ebook #13645, Project Gutenberg, 5 October 2005, www.ped .muni.cz/weng/outline_of_english_fiction/works/tatler/tatler_vol1.pdf (accessed 6 October 2006).

Discussion Guide

1. See Amit Goswami and others, *The Self Aware Universe: How Consciousness Creates the Material World* (New York: Putnam, 1993), 105–12.

Appendix A

1. For more on this, see Bernardo Olivera Osco, "Maturity and Generation: The Spiritual Formation of Young People," *Spiritus: A Journal of Christian Spirituality,* Spring 2003, 43.
2. See Amos Yong, *Beyond the Impasse* (Grand Rapids: Baker Academic, 2003), 190.

To learn more about WaterBrook Press and view
our catalog of products, log on to our Web site:
www.waterbrookpress.com

WATERBROOK
PRESS